Planning and Organising Business Functions

Other books by Stuart Turner:

Buying and Renovating a Cottage
Drive It! The Complete Book of Rallying

Planning and Organising Business Functions

Stuart Turner

Gower

Published by
Gower Publishing Company Limited
Aldershot, Hants, England

British Library Cataloguing in Publication Data

Turner, Stuart
    Planning and organising business functions.
    1. Congresses and conventions
    I. Title
    658.4'56   AS6   73079

ISBN 0 566 02394 6

Printed and bound in Great Britain by
Redwood Burn Limited, Trowbridge, Wiltshire

Contents

v

Preface

In recent years there has been a communications explosion and meetings and conferences are now an integral part of company life. But, too often, functions are held for traditional rather than business reasons and standards of organisation vary wildly.

The way you organise a function speaks volumes about your company. If an event is chaotic with faulty microphones and rambling speakers, the audience will conclude that the company is equally chaotic. This does not mean that every function has to be a show business production with dancing girls and special lighting – far from it – but at least the same thought should go into organising a function as goes into any other important aspect of a business. This book has been written to help in the process.

In order to illustrate all the ramifications of organising functions, it often quotes the 'ideal', describing large venues and elaborate programmes. Obviously, not everyone's financial or manpower resources (or needs for that matter) will stretch to such heights, but the principles, the importance of planning and attention to detail remain the same whatever the size of the event.

Stuart Turner

1 Basics

Any function, whether a small get-together or a major conference, should be planned with the same care that you would devote to any other aspect of your company's business. So the first thing to do is to establish your objectives. What are you really trying to achieve? Are you holding a function to impart information, to launch a new product or to motivate staff? What message do you wish to put across? Do you want any information to flow back to the company? (Unhappily this is too rarely the case.) There can be some benefit for a company if staff meet regularly because it helps to build team spirit, but if this seems to be the only reason for planning a meeting, then cancel it. Unless you have clear objectives for holding a meeting, the advice is simple: don't.

The audience will be covered in more detail in a later chapter, but at an early stage in your planning you need to consider the type of audience because, to some extent, it will determine the sort of meeting you hold, while the numbers will obviously affect your budget.

First, decide who are your prime targets. Are they the

1

sales force, the dealers, or customers? If you have to reach more than one audience at a series of meetings, invite them in the right order. For instance, you should show dealers a new product before customers, and before the media, although the time gap should not be too long otherwise word of a product announcement may leak out.

Having established your audience, next consider timing. Don't be too rigid. If you always hold a conference in March it would clearly be absurd to do so if you were about to introduce a new product a few weeks later.

Some industries have work peaks and it would be unwise to plan a conference for the middle of one of them. Equally, it would be foolish during a peak selling time for your product, because if your field force and/or dealers are away or distracted for a key period then sales could be affected. Don't plan a meeting or conference when maximum effort is needed elsewhere.

Conferences organised by companies as profit-making ventures (seminars on obscure EEC legislation will clearly be a growth industry) are not covered specifically in this book, although most of the principles apply and such functions need even more detailed planning. You must ensure that you are giving value for money and you may have the additional cost of advertising, direct mail shots, leaflet printing etc. Organising money-making conferences is a growth industry and almost seems to have created a special type of 'conference goer'. Attending a conference on an obscure topic is an elegant, though often unproductive, way of spending a day out of the office. Incidentally, certain conferences may attract sales people more anxious to reach the other delegates than learn anything – maybe they should be charged more.

Having settled your objectives and your basic messages and got a rough idea of the audience, you can now give some thought to the form your meeting or conference should take. It is important to decide what mood you are trying to project. Is it a morale-boosting session because the company is going through a lean time, or is it to encourage people to scale even higher peaks? Are you going to use the stick or carrot? (Remember that too much use of the stick may become counter-productive.) Is it to be an elegant, formal occasion or more of a relaxed get-together for the lads? Don't sneer at the latter because a feeling of belonging to a friendly group can be as important as (and better remembered than) a series of lectures. Remember that many companies operate efficiently not, as directors delude themselves, because of their carefully laid down systems but because of the informal underground network of contacts built up over drinks after meetings.

At an early stage in your planning you should consider what speeches, lectures or presentations are to be given – too often they seem designed just to fill in the time between meals. The more important the message you have to impart, the less razzmatazz you may need; if you are halving the retail prices of your products (or halving your workforce for that matter) people will remember the message without having a stage filled with dancing girls. But beware – if you have a new wonder product to launch and just thrust it in front of an audience without any build-up, they may think that you are indifferent towards it. You need to strike a careful balance so that people remember the message and the enthusiastic flavour of the presentation, without the latter dominating their thoughts.

On a less glamorous plane, it is a sad fact that many formal and association lectures contribute little to the fund of human knowledge because they simply feature old material warmed up. Aim higher for your meetings and remember the early advice: if you have nothing to say, why hold a meeting to say it? Do plan ahead and sow seeds for the next meeting so that you can refer back and prove that you intended something all along. For example, if the next three months look like being very difficult someone should make a clear reference to the fact, so that in six months' time they can say 'as we mentioned to you at the Brighton Conference, we were facing difficult times'.

Just because the managing director or board operate on a high cultural plane or enjoy formal dinners, don't assume that delegates will; tailor things to your audience, not to your social ambitions. If your company has been running conferences and meetings in a certain form and style for several years, that in itself may be a very good reason for changing; although be careful if you are organising something for a professional body – they can be rather zealous in guarding their traditions. If in doubt, be brave; business tends to be far too conservative.

Aim to organise things with style, but without going over the top. If you introduce too many show business features or have clearly spent an excessive amount of money, it may become counter-productive because you can actually turn an audience off by over-kill.

Do watch the 'escalation factor'. There may be a tendency to say 'we took the retailers to the Bahamas for a conference last year, this time we'd better go to Australia'. That route means you end up trying to take people to the moon; get back to basics by starting from a lower base. If you get into a mad race to outspend the competition you may simply be aiding the hotel and travel business. You should watch intra-company rivalry too. If one division of a company takes their fieldforce to an exotic place, it doesn't follow that other sections should automatically go abroad or spend more money on their meetings.

By this stage of your planning, a theme for the function may have emerged. For instance, if the meeting is an incentive trip abroad (the rules should be absolutely clear to avoid dissent) then you may carry a theme through the promotion. If you are selling fridges you could take people to the North Pole or the Equator and design your rules and letters of invitation accordingly.

Once a company has clarified its very broad aims, it is important to establish who is going to organise the function. Should it be Personnel, Marketing, Public Relations, Sales or. . . ? It will partly depend on the audience because departments may rightly feel that each should look after its own, and for small meetings this will invariably be the case. However, there is some merit in having one specialist in a company to organise functions and thus build up a bank of knowledge. Appointing a special 'task force' for each event rather smacks of panic.

If more than one department is involved, co-ordination between them is vital to avoid an overlap and clash of styles. It follows that any in-house organiser needs to be able to work with people and it helps if he (or she – the conference world has few problems with sex discrimination and some of the best producers are female) doesn't take 'no' too easily. It may also help if someone has a knowledge of learning methods and practices.

A company should not nominate a function organiser then forget him. Regular briefings are essential, although whoever is put in charge must *be* in charge. He must have enough authority to be able to dissuade people from changing slides or rearranging the order of speakers five minutes before a meeting starts (not the most effective way of putting over a message), and he must have the strength to play devil's advocate. If the sales manager gets excited over a 0.1 per cent rise in the market share of your product, he should be bold enough to point out that this does not justify a mounted charge across the stage by the Household Cavalry!

The organiser should be given adequate back-up – secretarial assistance etc., preferably with access to a word processor.

To assist internal communications, minutes should be kept of all meetings with an 'action by' column and, as an event of any size approaches, a worksheet or conference book should be prepared so that everyone knows who is doing what and when. If there are several company VIPs at the function, it should be clear just who is in charge, with deputies in mind for the key organisers in case of illness.

Using outside organisers

Let us be quite clear: organising a simple meeting or conference should not be beyond the skills of the average company but, because of workload problems or nervousness, you may decide that it is all too much and that you need outside help.

Many advertising and marketing magazines run regular features on conference organisation with lists of addresses, although probably the best way to find an outside company is by word of mouth or personal experience. If you attend a function which appears to be well run, consider asking that organiser to quote for your function. As with advertising agents or any other consultants, you must give an outside organisation a proper brief. They will want to know the obvious things – date, size of audience etc. – but, in addition, try to give them the 'flavour' of what you are trying to achieve. Make it clear whether you want them to create and arrange the whole thing or simply interpret your ideas and, in fairness, warn them of anything to avoid, e.g. the managing director is allergic to certain television presenters.

Get two or three quotations and sort out in advance if rejection fees will be charged for work in preparing a presentation which is unsuccessful. Watch the ethics of the business; don't steal ideas from company *B*'s presentation and then give the work to company *A*.

Try not to be too impressed if an organising company plays a showreel of former triumphs for you; it may be effective, but remember that the techniques for launching a soap powder may not be quite right to introduce an expectant world to your new multi-purpose sludge dispersant.

Any organisation can call itself a 'conference organiser' so be quite objective when selecting an outside company to act for you. Audiovisual (AV), lasers and many other special effects are available and feasible and their producers may make it all sound very exciting. So it may be, but keep your head.

When vetting an outside agency, does it show signs of being organised on businesslike lines, with people in charge of different aspects of the work? It should have some semblance of internal discipline, although when you are dealing with a creative area don't be surprised if some staff turn up for meetings in jeans and sandals. Some companies will claim they need very long lead times, certainly so for a major conference, but they should also be flexible enough to modify something at the last minute if a change of circumstances affects your business.

A successful function hinges on people and you must be

able to get on with the staff in the organising company. Don't plump for a company or director who automatically agrees with everything you say; you want ideas people not yes-men. You do not need a consultant who tries to disguise problems, nor do you want one who cheerfully gossips about, or knocks, the opposition because it will be your turn next. There is some advantage in sticking to one company because you will get to know them, they will get to know you and a rapport may build up so that, for instance, helpful comparisons may be made that you both understand. For example, the hotel in X is about the same standard as the one we used last year in Y. However, don't get too cosy – call in other companies to quote from time to time.

Having chosen a company to organise your function, be quite clear about the terms of payment, what their fees cover and cancellation charges should you have to abort the function. Be equally clear about the lines of communication. Discourage them from lobbying your chairman or directors if the proper liaison point should be lower down the company tree.

Alternatives

Before you sign the agreement with a conference organising company, or book a lot of hotel rooms, ask yourself: 'Is the meeting really necessary?' Gathering an audience together for a function costs time and money. Are there any alternatives? Well, delegates could stay on their own premises and cluster round telexes or computers and hold an electronic conference, but there would not be much life in that.

Simple telephone links may serve instead of meetings for many purposes. These will become more common when view-phones are readily available and people can see who they are talking to.

You could make video tapes of your speakers and mail them to district offices or retail outlets for people to sit and watch, but this would not count as a conference, for there would be no conferring. Nevertheless, such a video, particularly if it featured much detailed information, could augment a national meeting.

In the UK British Telecom has half a dozen venues which can be linked up for a video conference and additional links are available to some continental countries. Perhaps worth trying for small groups?

Or you could organise a video conference with proceedings televised live to other venues by satellite. Clearly this moves away from being an in-house project, and would need experts to secure satellite time and supply the equipment. Incidentally, at any function using links to other venues, speakers should be encouraged to look into the cameras as well as at their live audiences so that people at other venues will feel part of the proceedings.

Conferences using satellite links tend to be sharper than more conventional meetings because they have to be carefully structured and thus encourage people to stick to their subjects and not waffle. There is also the flexibility of bringing in local experts for a few minutes who would not want to travel to a distant function.

If you move into all this high technology it may save your delegates time but, at the moment, costs will still be high. Nevertheless, if you pull off an effective meeting using modern technology, you will be indicating to people that yours is an up-to-date, modern company. In the future, with huge television screens, three-dimensional techniques etc., we will see a dramatic growth in satellite conferences, although they may never have quite the same flavour as a function where people meet face to face. To prevent art and high technology from taking over totally, it will be vital for companies to go back to their basic training and keep asking: what are our objectives?

2 Finance

Proper budgeting is essential for any function. It is easy to get carried away and overspend, particularly if you are far away from base, the sun is shining and there is a handy bar. An important event may warrant a separate cost centre and a cash flow forecast, and for an overseas function it could pay to have a full-time finance man along to look after the coffers. He may tend to splutter at some of the costs (e.g. for hiring star entertainers), but by playing devil's advocate he should at least be able to cover his own expenses and more.

Take into account the real costs to the company of a function and also the hidden ones, such as expenses put on individual expense account forms by company delegates. Discuss with the company's finance people how extras at hotels should be paid. It seems absurd to have delegates queueing at the hotel to pay for extras such as breakfasts and phone calls, only to charge them via their individual expense accounts later. Much simpler to pay them all as a lump sum – but that's accountants for you.

The important thing is to list everything in your budgeting. For example, if you are putting bowls of fruit in delegates' rooms as they check into the hotel, then itemise the expense in your budget. Spell out to delegates exactly what is, and what is not, free.

Do allow for contingencies when preparing a budget. The managing director, flushed from a successful speech, may keep the bar open longer than budgeted. Remember that things like overnight slide-making can be very expensive. Include an amount for any 'cash inducements' you may need to get material moved or union hassles resolved; don't expect receipts for such transactions.

Obviously your budget will be governed by the number of delegates for your function. This can present problems with, for instance, press conferences when you are never sure how many people are going to turn up. The only thing you can do is budget on the high side.

Your budget should be split between fixed and variable costs. Fixed costs are those that you have to meet regardless of how many people turn up – organising costs, security, room charges, printing, hire of equipment, projectionist etc. Variable costs will include those related to each delegate – meals etc. If you have chartered planes for an overseas function and there are spare seats, the variable cost of taking extra people will only be the hotel and food plus, if it is a company employee, their lost time at work. Costs will not necessarily be less for smaller meetings because you will have to make the same number of phone calls to book venues etc.

When budgeting, allow for reconnaissance visits to venues. If you find you have to take a window out to get display material in, allow for the cost. Remember that there may be additional charges, e.g. if you have to book the venue a day or two in advance to build a stage, or if you need security people on guard overnight to protect your exhibits. For overseas venues, keep in mind currency fluctuations and the best time to pay bills.

Put things in writing to suppliers, venues and outside organisers. People in the conference world who have kindly read a draft of this book have all suggested that this point should be re-emphasised so, however relaxed your relationship may be and however much business you do over the phone, *put things in writing*. Even if a conference is a wild success, the euphoria will evaporate and when accounts come to be paid you need the written record. Who owns any props? Can they be reused? If you have several exhibitions or conferences during a year, using the same material can help to amortise the cost. Everyone must be clear just who can authorise additional expenditure. It is unfair to penalise others because your accounts system results in slow payment. Remember that you may want to go back to a venue and they may not exactly welcome you if they had to wait a long time for their money after your last visit.

When you have drawn up a realistic budget, consider carefully whether it is all worthwhile. It may be difficult to evaluate the cost effectiveness of a function because many of the benefits (a cross flow of ideas, new contacts etc.) are inevitably subjective. Whatever you do, the function must reflect your company style, so if your budgeting shows that Bali is stretching things too far, then settle for Bournemouth and do it properly. It is better to cut back and do a small, shorter event well, than to stretch things so that there is no second glass of wine at dinner.

Financial traffic need not be all one way. If you can prove that there is some training involved in the function, or it is an export exhibition, various grants may be available. You may consider charging your delegates but if, for instance, you charge your own retailers to attend one of your overseas functions, the cannier ones may compare your costs with those of a travel agent. You may damage relationships if they feel that you are overcharging them to cover your own company expenses out of their fees.

If you are charging, consider discounts for early registration so that you can get your plans laid earlier and also have a cut-off point after which no refund is possible. Needless to say, you must clarify cancellation charges with hotels, transport, suppliers etc. Have the wit to cancel rather than end up with a lukewarm affair offering poor value for money through lack of atmosphere. You can pack a function with a certain number of company people but, if you overdo this, other delegates will realise what you are doing.

Another way of helping your cash flow may be to allow suppliers to put on an exhibition aimed at your audience, in return for a contribution to costs; don't hustle too hard along this road.

Tax implications

You must check the tax implications if you are organising a function for which there is some element of reward (say for beating sales targets), particularly one involving overseas travel. Delegates won't thank you if they get an unexpected tax demand later. You have to accept one basic fact – not many taxmen go on glamorous overseas trips as part of their jobs, so don't expect too much sympathy.

If you include a few lectures and a business visit (say to a factory) on an overseas trip so that you can claim fairly genuine business reasons, you may get some relief. It may also be possible for the organising company to settle tax centrally (paying at the basic rate direct to their local tax office) or even contribute to delegates' tax expenses. The position is changing and it is not easy to get a clear ruling. The safest thing to do is consult then keep delegates and the taxmen in the picture. It is important that you, as the company, are not seen to be indulging in tax evasion. For the same reason, you should get the latest guidance on the position over VAT.

Insurance

With the high costs of running a major function, you should obviously take out appropriate insurance. The most sensible protection is to run financial checks on the companies you propose to deal with because there have been well publicised failures among travel and tour operators and even production companies. In addition to such checks, you should take out adequate insurance so that you are covered against the following various disasters which can befall you:

* Damage to the venue. Establish the position with the owners because it would seem unrealistic that, say, you should have to pay if his faulty roof falls in on your delegates.
* Rain, if your event is held outdoors.
* Negligence, for example if you bring in a pop group and they wreck the place.
* Non-appearance of a star speaker or performer, leaving you to find a last-minute substitute.
* An air strike, leaving you with hotels booked.
* Natural disasters (quite apart from those that you yourself inflict on your delegates).
* Loss or damage to property or equipment.
* Injury to delegates, such as falling over an unlit step.
* Loss of cash by delegates.
* Cancellation of the event.

For some of these things the venue owner's insurance may be extended to provide cover. The best advice is to consult your company insurance man if you have one, or a broker specialising in the conference business. By the way, it is easy to think that 'it can't happen', but with electrical cables, nails in timber, dim lighting and temporary structures, a function can be quite dangerous. Be covered.

3 Planning

Once you have worked out your objectives and finances, the detailed planning of your programme can begin and it will be influenced to a great extent by your 'customers' – the people you are trying to reach. Keep them in mind at all times; if you lose sight of your audience your function may fail.

Consider some of the following items about an audience:

* Boffins will cope with longer and more erudite sessions than we lesser mortals.

* Head office staff should not assume that the fieldforce or trade outlets have their detailed knowledge of the company, which is why it may be a good idea to put on a display of the latest company products at a function.

* If an important event is being organised for one audience, consider others at the same time. If you have a conference with a stunning reveal sequence aimed at retailers, why not show it to the workforce, union leaders,

community dignitaries, etc?
* If you have a series of meetings, get them in the right order. In general, information should flow downwards and you should tell senior people first, or they may be upset if they find out from subordinates. The only exception perhaps is to invite a less important group for the first showing of a complicated presentation, so that if it goes wrong it is not too big a disaster.
* Which groups mix? You may find from your own experience that delegates from certain parts of the country get on together well. Consider deliberately mixing people so that you get more cross-fertilisation of business ideas.
* Get the 'politics' right when drawing up invitation lists. If you leave someone out they may feel hurt and their omission may increase ·any feeling of 'them and us' which already exists in a company.
* If an overseas trip is a reward for a sales in- centive scheme, consider letting non- winners buy places on the trip (paying some or all of the cost depending how close they come to their targets). This may help to build up numbers, but a risk is that it may devalue the trip in the eyes of the winners.

International audiences

If you are organising an event for delegates of different nationalities bear in mind the following points:

* You may need to slow the pace of any presen- tations from that for a single-language audience, to allow for 'translation time'. Because people seem fluent in your language when chatting socially, it may be wrong to assume that the same applies when they are

coping with a long lecture. Some audiences may need simultaneous translation facilities (see Chapter 15).

* Take care that you do not cause offence by breaching local customs if holding a function abroad.
* Remember that custom and practice over punctuality, start times, meal times etc. may differ in other countries.
* You may get a cool reception in some countries if you don't use their national airline to move delegates.
* Allow for jet lag.
* Don't make the schedule for your function too tight if you have an international audience – the cross-fertilisation through social contact will be more important than at a purely domestic affair.
* Above all, don't patronise foreigners!

Partners

'Stag' occasions must eventually, and mercifully, die, but one decision you may have to take is whether to invite delegates' wives to your function and, as more women climb the business tree, husbands too. You may even have to decide what to do if someone wants to bring along a partner of the same sex, although for a few years yet I suspect they would have to feel very confident of their career prospects before doing so. Certainly any large group is likely to include unmarried partners. It is best to turn a blind eye but at least be aware of the possibilities in your planning.

It would be crudely tactless to attempt to make it compulsory for wives to attend a company function. Those who are businesswomen in their own right would quickly, and rightly, tell you what to do with your conference. Your aim should be to organise your event so well that people want to attend. Wives will want clear guidance on dress and you must accept the risk that some may drink a little too much and speak a lot too freely, which may not be such a bad thing if the bosses have the wit to listen.

Having partners present may dilute the level of knowledge, and therefore interest, in your subject. For example, if 5 per cent of the audience are local dignitaries and 50 per cent of the rest are wives or girlfriends, you are actually preaching to quite a small number, so presentations should not go into heavy detail.

Nevertheless, if partners do attend, they should be given all the conference material so that they feel totally involved, but not to the extent that you harangue poor sales performers in front of wives. Some slick sales manuals may recommend this, but it does seem like appalling industrial relations.

On the plus side, partners need not double costs because often single delegates will be occupying twin-bedded rooms. But do be clear on costs – delegates must know what is at their own expense.

If there are free days in your programme (and there should be if you've taken people to some exotic place) guide your guests on what is available, possibly with a 'what to do' desk in the hotel foyer; visits to fresh attractions, such as a newly opened museum or theme park that has been in the news, will be well received. Plan special entertainment for wives when husbands are involved in particularly heavy conference sessions. Perhaps put on a special session for them on how they can help in the business; a visit to the kitchens with talks by the hotel chef; coach tours, fashion shows, visits to show houses or local stores. The list of possibilities depends on your imagination and what is available locally. The suggestions sound desperately patronising, but they work.

If delegates bring partners then the party will be unbalanced unless company hosts bring partners too.

The programme

Having established the make-up of your audience, you can

plan the overall programme for your function. The pace should reflect the mood you are trying to project – short, sharp lectures and a brisk pace for a highly motivating conference, a more relaxed and reflective mood if you have other objectives. Incidentally, although functions are usually organised for the highest of motives, the information in-take may rarely be very high – delegates who regard your conference as a relaxed day out of the shop, may resent being asked to do too much hard work.

Get a broad feel for the balance of your programme, pencilling in what presentations, reveals and so on you want and then fill in the details. Try to keep it lively. Three hours in a smoke-filled room is not conducive to good learning so even a sales meeting with a dozen attending should include a break for people to stretch their legs. Other points to bear in mind are as follows:

*   If you are to get any messages across, your audience must be ready to listen and their threshold of boredom will be low if the seats are uncomfortable, the slides poor and the atmosphere heavy.
*   Two breaks in a session are better than one, although they will take longer.
*   If you have inherited the organisation of a function with clearly laid down traditions, it may be sensible to stick to them (at least for the first year) provided they have not become too moribund.
*   Consider a theme for your function. For example, if it is a conference to launch a new razor, invite guests to come unshaven and let them try the new wonder product.
*   Build in working sessions where appropriate. Split your audience into groups of a dozen or so, or you won't get any cross-fertilisation. Only you will know whether your audience will put up with in-tray exercises and the like.

Above all in your planning try to pace the programme so that you are always in control without regimenting the audience. For example, don't put tough sessions after long journeys nor encourage very late nights before a key day, but do build up to a key speech or lecture so that the mood is right. Delegates should be encouraged to expect the big occasion, which means that you shouldn't put a key speech immediately after lunch, the time for something lightweight. Avoid leaving your big news until the very end of your function – delegates may need time to talk over a complicated point with their colleagues. This advice does not preclude you from ending with important but brief news, such as that expense allowances are being doubled.

Speakers

Should you use company staff or show business personalities to present your message, say at a major conference? Company members should, if possible, be chosen on their ability to deliver a presentation, not on their pecking order in the company ranks. The in-house organiser may need tact in this area.

Be careful if you get involved with show business personalities to make presentations. They may be more interested in projecting their personalities than your product and some are fairly self important and will attempt to dominate proceedings. Half-known actors may leave your audience puzzling where they have seen them rather than remembering your message.

Obviously your cheapest speaker will be an in-house one and a panel of company experts to answer questions may be a low-cost way of adding a little sparkle to your function. Don't have too many on a panel – five is the working maximum, i.e. two on each side of a chairman. The chairman should not expect every panellist to answer every question, nor should he allow them to start private chats. There should be some questions 'planted' in the audience to break the ice in case of a slow start. A galaxy of top company VIPs may be inhibiting. The chairman should have enough personality to handle awkward or silly questions.

When looking for a single outside speaker or lecturer to lift your function, do keep things in perspective. If you have a small gathering of, say, twelve trade customers, don't expect a well-known politician to fly half way round the world to address them. In fact, be wary of politicians anyway. Instead of an address tailored to your group, you may simply get a party political broadcast and politicians of any creed grinding axes can grate. There will be some kudos to your company if you find an unknown speaker who is brilliant. Famous speakers will lift an audience's expectations and get the adrenalin going, although the let down will be greater if they prove poor. Don't book a successful speaker for a second time too soon, or you may get a repeat of much of the same material.

Word-of-mouth is probably the best way of finding a speaker. If you, or one of your colleagues, have heard someone speak well, then get after him, either direct or via the company organising the function or through an agency. If you book a celebrity, such as a television star, through an agency the contract may say 'professional engagements permitting'. However, if someone has to pull out of your function because he lands a major role, a reputable agency should guarantee to find you a substitute.

Commendably, you may love your company, but there is no reason why outsiders should too, so you must expect to pay speakers and if you have famous names in mind, they will not be cheap.

If you have had a rather lavish morning show then consider a serious speaker after lunch to flatter your audience by giving them, say, an erudite look into the future. Economists are always a safe bet because no-one ever checks later to see if their forecasts were nonsense.

Once you have found a speaker, you must put things in writing. Do get names right and if you have booked a distinguished speaker keep an eye on the Honours List in case your choice is elevated before your function. He may be hurt if you have not noticed.

If a speaker is to perform well he (and all the 'hes' could be 'shes', of course) must be properly informed. Your briefing letter to a speaker should include some or all of the following:

* Day and date (quote both to avoid mistakes).
* Type of event, e.g. conference, after lunch/ dinner speech.
* Venue (with special directions for finding if difficult).
* Name and telephone number of contact in your company.
* Type of dress, e.g. informal or black tie.
* Whether a room has been booked for changing or staying.
* Start time (be realistic – speakers will hate hanging around because you were optimistic on this).
* Size of audience and whether mixed or stag; type of audience (age, background etc.).
* Running order of speeches/lectures and who else will be speaking.
* Whether the speaker is proposing/respond- ing to any toast.
* Length of speech.
* Whether the press will be present.
* Any equipment available/needed.
* Plus any other points relevant to your function.

Guide speakers on how ribald they can be and remember that planning in the cold light of day may make you forget what your reps are like after a few glasses of wine with a meal.

Delegate someone in the company to look after your speaker. Telephone him near the date on some pretext or other to check that he still has you in his diary, particularly if the booking was made many months ahead. Your contingency plan should include understudies for key speakers and if a VIP drops out you must make the excuse convincing or the audience will be offended.

Watch the running order of speakers. If you book a superb speaker, put him on last in fairness to the others – don't fire your big gun first leaving other speakers shell shocked.

Don't expect speakers to come to your briefing meetings unless you are prepared to pay them twice. Obtain biographies of speakers but don't embarrass them by reading out whole reams of information; you need just enough to establish the speaker's credentials. Finally, whatever speaker you have, see that they get home safely, perhaps by someone running them to a station or airport; write to thank them afterwards and send them any press cuttings generated by their performance.

You may need one other speaker at your function, that is a senior guest or company official to say 'thank you'. Pick this person with care otherwise you will offend those not chosen. The person selected may need to be briefed not to go on too long, nor to grind any individual axes. Civic dignitaries rarely impress anyone except themselves as speakers, although it may be tactful to invite them to say a few words.

Other entertainment

This sub-heading assumes, hopefully, that at least some of your speakers have been entertaining, but if you are looking for other means to lift your function, such as at a gala dinner in the middle of a conference, then it must be in harmony otherwise it will jar. For example, someone from your company should see a cabaret act before you book it; don't take the word of an agent or hotel. If in doubt,avoid acts that are too subtle or slow moving and remember that you will be regarded as a smart organiser if you pick a young star on the way up, rather than a fading one on the way down. An act should be given a proper introduction and build-up, and be briefed just as carefully as you would any other person taking part. For example, a jazz singer might like to know whether the audience is the equivalent of coach parties or jazz aficionados. Check that the piano in the venue has been tuned.

Inevitably, any dolly birds or models used during presentations at business conferences will be regarded as 'entertainment' so they should be pleasant to look at. If yours is an up-market organisation then clearly you should hire cool, elegant, well-dressed girls.

Before leaving 'other entertainment' I am reminded that some paternalistic firms have their own company songs to entertain and motivate people. No thank you!

Planning postscript

Having sketched out the programme – the mix of lectures, speeches, entertainment etc. – try to judge if the balance is right, because this is the key to the success or failure of a function. So much depends on interlocking things; you may have been forced to change one ingredient and it may have affected others. However, once you have the balance settled to your satisfaction, retain enough flexibility to change if opportunities for improvement come up, e.g. if you find your venue has a lawn running down to a lake, then you may have a natural place for an evening cocktail party if the weather is kind.

4 Venues

The choice of venue can make or break a function, so give it considerable thought. If cost is a prime consideration, consider in-house venues. Do you have a training facility that could be used, or a large meeting room at head office? Both less glamorous perhaps than an outside venue, but cheaper and more convenient. Or do you have a new factory extension to be opened? Use the opportunity to let people see it. You may find that in-house caterers will welcome the challenge of putting on a special spread.

If you decide to move away from company premises, you will have a wide choice – conferences in particular are big business and there is keen competition for the work. Towns like the idea of relatively high spenders hitting them and Britain in particular is almost in danger of having too many major conference complexes; in theory, if you move to a professional conference venue they should know what they are doing and you should not be troubled by extraneous noises or poor acoustics, but don't count on theory – double check just the same. Most functions still use more traditional hotel venues and here again there is a wide choice. But you need to take care over your selection. Browse through the standard travel trade books of venues, but be slightly wary of hotel brochures because they can be as misleading as estate agents' particulars. The promotional abilities of some venues have outstripped reality; it is a lot easier to produce a slick brochure than house 500 people efficiently.

If you need to hold meetings in different parts of the country, remember that your fieldforce may have ideas on which hotels may be suitable in their area.

When you have a rough list of suitable venues it is worth sending someone on a whistlestop tour. Your company rules may, perhaps rightly, prohibit facility trips, i.e. with expenses paid by the hotels, but you must visit a new venue before booking it for a function of any importance. If your company sells to hotels then, clearly, it makes sense to spread your business around your main customers but, above all, your choice should be governed by the image you are trying to project. Be realistic. If your retailers are rowdy, avoid elegant venues with priceless antiques. The best hotel will be one well used to business meetings and conferences, so avoid traditional hotels which have not updated their ideas. You don't want somewhere stuffy and decaying with no double glazing or air conditioning.

Although popular venues may need to be booked well in advance most hotels will be glad of your business, particularly out of season, so if anywhere seems less than enthusiastic, move on. Don't accept a promise that a venue can 'lift' itself out of its class; it is unlikely to be able to do so. Similarly, be slightly wary of venues that are not regularly used for meetings and conferences, because their organisational cracks may show.

The following points should also be considered:

* The size of your group is critical – will you take over the venue completely? Conference delegates and other guests sometimes form an uneasy mix.
* Are there other functions on at the same time? If so, is there any security or business clash? Will too many functions at the same

time stretch the hotel's resources? In particular, beware of another function in a room under or adjacent to yours, because of the possibility of distracting noise.

* Can the hotel cope if you are a large group? Will it be able to handle the demand for meals and unusual requests, such as snacks at midnight for the staff who are working late to put a presentation together? Does it insist on jackets and ties being worn in the restaurant? Commendable perhaps to maintain standards, but it may cause problems for a production crew (the 'workers' tend to favour jeans and T-shirts).

* If you are using a venue out of season, e.g. in winter at a traditional summer resort, will there be adequate staff? Will laundry facilities cope?

* When you visit a hotel, ask to see the worst bedroom as well as an average one and check if there are enough rooms, with bathrooms.

* Are suites available for VIPs who may need to hold private meetings? You may, of course, have company rules to juggle with, covering what standard of rooms certain management levels are allowed.

* Are any of your guests handicapped? If so, check access doors, ramps etc.

* Are there enough lifts? Old hotels may not have been modernised in this respect. You won't be popular if your delegates are stranded on various floors as a cocktail party gets underway. Are there service lifts? If not, luggage movement may clog the passenger lifts.

* What is access like from public roads? Is there a reasonable unloading area for cars, and ample parking? You may even need to check if there is a convenient helicopter landing pad. Remember that when people leave their

cars (or helicopters) they need signs to the venue. These direction signs will be the first thing they see of you, so they should be smart.

* If delegates are arriving by plane or train, are there adequate taxis?

* Is there a 'house engineer' – someone who can handle lighting, etc., at the venue – or is it left to whoever happens to have a screwdriver handy when something goes wrong?

* Is there a TV relay system in the bedrooms and, if so, could it be used to show a company video to delegates? (This does rather smack of Big Brother so, whatever you do, don't set exams on the video later.)

If possible avoid hotels where delegates are totally marooned. They may like to stroll to local shops, for instance; the only exception is an hotel in the middle of a golf course.

If possible, observe a similar sized function to the one you are planning at the venue so that you can check it under pressure; at the very least call anonymously at a busy time for a test meal. One simple test is to ask for a glass of water at the start of a meal; often it arrives with the coffee, or not at all. Do waiters get orders right when they serve you or do they have to keep asking 'Are you the fried plaice?'. Does the hotel appear to have staff problems? A warning sign. If yours is an up-market affair, do the serving staff wear gloves? They are slightly more attractive than broken finger nails.

The quality of the cutlery and crockery may be a good guide, and the general air of the place should tell you whether it will be right for your function. Small details count. Do the serving trolleys squeak? They shouldn't.

Above all, when you visit, check if there is a conference manager or someone in charge of functions. If not, move on, because the receptionist or car park attendant is unlikely to be able to handle your function efficiently as a part-time job.

Bear in mind that the bigger hotel groups move staff around; if you find a really good manager it could be worth following him around with your function, because the attitude of hotel staff can be as important as the ambience; they must be co-operative if your conference is to function properly. Make sure that there will be sufficient skilled waiters/waitresses for your event because slow service can spoil things. Establish who will be responsible for your function on the day and ensure that he or she will have absolute authority to deal with awkward staff, or a crisis in the kitchen etc. And know where he or she can be found on the day. Don't stand any nonsense or put up with half promises because hotels need the business; you are paying and should insist on things being run your way. Let me repeat: if your function is to work well you will need total co-operation from the hotel, so it is worth making yourself known to the head waiter if you are organising a meal and come to a 'mutually satisfactory arrangement' about co-operation on the day, in other words, tips.

Vetting a function room

Although the general flavour of an hotel is important, you should pay most attention to the particular room to be used for your function – whether it be a meeting, conference or full blown banquet and whether it be in a five-star hotel or a warehouse.

You should walk around the room you propose to use for example to decide where speakers should be placed. Are any pillars going to block the view in certain places?

Can the room be found easily? Always have a supply of free-standing signs as well as stick-on company decals so that the delegates can be directed properly.

Is the venue big enough? Can it cope with your numbers without becoming too crowded? You don't want a room half empty because it will look cold, but if your guests are constantly banging elbows, it will not be very relaxing and if the weather is warm, everyone will get hot, sticky and unhappy and less able to concentrate.

The ideal may be an 'elastic' room composed of several interconnecting sections, where one section may be used as a start, and extended to a second or third if more invitations are accepted than expected. Such linked rooms are also useful if you want a reception area for coffee, then somewhere for a meeting before moving into a third room for a meal. Caution though, if you are only using part of such a facility check that the folding walls are soundproof, because if there is a function next to yours, you could have problems. I once called for questions at a forum in such a venue at which point, as if on cue, a band struck up at a wedding reception in the adjacent section, and totally wrecked our function. Not unnaturally, the groom was not prepared to postpone things for us.

Venues such as cinemas and theatres often have their own built-in elasticity because you can block off a balcony until the main hall is full. If you only intend to use part of a facility, block off the other seats neatly with strips of cloth. Bare seats may make it look as if your function has flopped.

The ideal room will be soundproof, although you will not find this very often. However, at least consider the acoustics. A long, thin room is not ideal because hearing can be difficult at the back while, as a general rule, rooms with metal girders and perhaps steel walls (such as workshops) are poor and can become a nightmare when trying to place loudspeakers.

Is the ceiling high enough for a screen? Unhappily screens are rarely placed high enough – watch the craning necks next time you go to a film or slide show at a function. The screen must be as high as possible – it is better that those at the front get stiff necks from looking up, than those at the back can't see at all.

Can the room be blacked out? Remember if you vet a venue in the winter for a booking in June the evenings won't be so dark then.

Check the seats; their comfort is critical because the mind won't absorb facts if it is bothered by numb nether regions. If you are stuck with hard seats, at least try to give plenty of leg room so that guests can wriggle about, and build in more coffee breaks or other pauses to give them some relief.

People will not concentrate on a presenter or new

product unless they can see. Tiered seats are perhaps the best, but you are unlikely to find them very often. If you have your own tiered seating built from scaffolding, watch that things can't drop through the slats, either distracting the audience with the clatter or injuring those beneath. Is there a stage available or will you have to build something? Any stage must be strong enough for your purposes. Do you need a special stage such as a cat walk for a fashion show? If you are putting on a display in a coffee area, will the floor take the weight? Will your exhibits go through the door?

The following further points should be considered when vetting a room for a function:

* Is the electricity supply adequate? You will need three-phase with up to 60 amps per phase if you are using a large amount of lighting.
* How flexible is the lighting? Are there dimmer switches?
* Is the water supply adequate? If yours is a lavish show with laser beams, you will need water for cooling.
* Is the room noisy? If so, find somewhere else. Whatever you do, never hold a function in a room with a bar because the noise will be too distracting. If there is a public address system which may be helpful at times to call delegates, can it be switched off? You must be able to silence it, otherwise a stray announce-ment is bound to destroy the mood of your meeting.
* Is the heating easily controlled? Is there air conditioning and, if so, is it quiet? If none, open windows may introduce the noises you are trying to avoid.
* Are there adequate and well signposted cloakroom and toilet facilities? Insist that roller towels are renewed regularly.
* If windows and doors are noisy, ask for them to be oiled. If a floorboard squeaks, you may

not be able to do much about it, but at least avoid the spot if speakers have to walk to and from a lectern.

* Does the hotel have a rack for display literature?

* Do you need special extension telephone lines for a computer?

* Is there a place for a message board for delegates, and does the venue offer secretarial services plus a photocopier, telex etc? If you are planning to use the venue's projection equipment, check it. Don't rely on pulling something out of a dusty cupboard at the last minute and making it work. Remember that you can hire almost anything.

* Try to remember the small things. Is there a block and gavel for a chairman? Is there a hairdresser for women delegates? If you need a toastmaster, does the venue know of a good local one?

* Are smoke detectors installed in the room? You may need to watch this point, otherwise your stirring hell, fire and thunder sequence, with smoke effects, may set off alarms and empty the room before a keynote speech.

5 Unusual venues

An off-beat or unusual venue may ensure a strong turnout of guests, if it intrigues their curiosity, and good press coverage, but don't be wildly original if it means that you become too off-beat for your audience. A nightclub atmosphere, for instance, could be daunting for a rather staid business group. But with only that proviso, there are countless opportunities for companies to use novel venues for functions of all types.

Trains

Trains offer advantages for some purposes such as exhibitions. You can take your exhibits to your audience, while avoiding the cost of setting up and taking down displays several times. You can put almost anything into a train that you can display at a static venue. There is usually car parking at stations and they are always easy to find.

Even if you don't use trains for functions, remember that moving delegates by train and feeding them en route will save time.

Ships

As with trains, you could move a presentation or exhibition to your audience by sailing round the coast or along a canal. If you cast off each time to add interest at least you will be assured of a captive audience, unless your guests get so desperate that they are prepared to swim to get away from your presentation.

For lavish conferences, you could consider one of the cruising liners.

Planes

Before using a plane, with its film facilities, as a conference venue, remember that some people are scared of flying while the unusual environment would perhaps hamper concentration. A 'plane conference' could prove quite expensive, but there is no reason why you should not show a company film on a chartered plane en route to an overseas function.

Educational establishments

Universities, agricultural colleges, colleges of further education, and many other places of learning, can present a perfect atmosphere if you are organising a specifically 'learning' conference, although they may be a bit spartan for other purposes. Universities are usually free for about two-fifths of the year, although the free times may not fit in with the dates you want.

Most educational places will quote for an inclusive package and usually their rooms are single which is ideal. They offer good lecture halls and recreational facilities and, above all, there is always plenty of space for registration.

Against all that, there will be little or no room service and possibly no colour TV. But is that the end of civilisation as we know it?

Catering can often be surprisingly good. I've had splendid dinners at conferences organised at four different British universities.

Theatres

Theatre owners are looking for ways to increase their revenue and will often make their premises available for a function.

If there is a regular show running it may be difficult to get into the theatre early enough if you have an elaborate set although, if appropriate, there is perhaps no reason why you shouldn't use the existing set for your presentation and perhaps some of the actors too.

At least with a theatre you will be saved the problem of having to put special seating into a venue and you may even find a revolving stage which can be used during a presentation for extra effect.

Sporting venues

Racecourses (horse, car and greyhound) as well as football and cricket clubs are just some of the sporting venues vying for conference business. Most such venues have good parking and are usually well signposted. Many will offer packages, linking attendance at a sporting event (or in the case of race tracks, driving a racing car) with your function. Beware – you want people to take away your message not the name of the winner of the third race.

Sports halls themselves tend to be too big and lack atmosphere and it is difficult to build any in unless you go to considerable expense with decoration.

Stately homes

Increasingly, the stately homes of England (and Wales and Scotland too) are looking for conference business, although few of them will be able to take very large numbers. In this category you can include castles (those in Scotland are particularly good) and museums. Give delegates a guidebook as a souvenir, but be careful with point-of-sale or other display material. It can look in poor taste if it is cluttering up a stately setting.

Remember that his lordship will probably do his party piece if the money is right. Stately homes may be particularly effective with delegates from abroad.

Other venues

You could use circuses (not inappropriate for some conferences) but tents or marquees need a firm floor and efficient heating unless you are quite sure of the weather. Modern modular tents with metal frames are good. Don't forget the cellars of inns, old gaols, zoos, or even a health farm – cut down on your food costs and tell delegates that you are doing it for their own good. The list is endless.

One final point to keep in mind with unusual venues: ensure that the necessary back-up facilities are available and of the right quality. The effect of holding a function in an elegant stately home will be marred if your seats for dinner are plastic stacking ones borrowed from a factory canteen.

6 Overseas venues

Think carefully before you decide to take your function abroad. Costs need not be much higher than at home, particularly out of season, but an overseas function will need a lot more organisation and there will be greater risks of something going wrong. Of course the rewards could be higher too, but don't go abroad just for the sake of it or because 'we went abroad last time'. It can be tiring in a plane and even short flights can slightly disorientate passengers. Some people don't like flying, while well-seasoned travellers have probably seen more than enough of places like Monte Carlo. Strong sunshine is not to everyone's taste and fighting off mosquitoes is not a bundle of fun. But, despite all this, if you are looking for excitement and a lift for your function, go abroad.

Study the time of year you are proposing to travel because although a holiday venue may be cheap for a function out of season, this may be because it is either impossibly hot or impossibly cold. Also inquire about rainfall for the time of year.

Don't over-regiment your delegates abroad, nor make

things over-complicated. You may have to adjust to a different pace. Local mealtimes may be different and siesta time after lunch may close everything down, while punctuality of staff may not be quite what you expect.

Reconnaissance of an overseas venue is vital unless you really know and trust your travel agent's judgement. Although you may have organised a function at home within the company, you will almost certainly need outside help in running an overseas function, perhaps from a conference organiser, certainly from a travel agent. Choosing a travel agent is not unlike selecting an advertising agency – the bigger ones are safer but less imaginative; the smaller ones are bolder but riskier.

Check all the things you would for a venue at home plus the following:

* Will the local power supply suit your equipment?
* If you are taking equipment, will there be problems in negotiating customs?
* What are the terms of payment at the hotel; are guests on *pension* or *demi-pension* ? If certain meals only are covered in the overall expense (ideally they should all be) a ticket scheme for meals is often more efficient than booking them to room numbers (which can introduce service delays).

It may be convenient to arrange for delegates to stay on for additional days at their own expense but you must spell out quite clearly when they start paying. If the second part of their stay goes sour, your function may be tarnished with the memory.

If you are travelling to an exciting venue, it makes sense to create the maximum impact so mail a glamorous brochure to delegates and, if it is an incentive involving wives, to home addresses. If your budget will stand it, a simple booklet on the country is a nice touch.

Here are some further points on overseas venues:

* You must have home telephone numbers of company personnel back at base. You may

need to contact them at odd times and it may be easier at weekends when telephones are quieter. You should also have telex numbers.

* A visit to a local branch or similar business to yours may seem a good idea when you plan it, but is unlikely to be popular if the weather is sensational when you get there. Guests will be more interested in relaxing, which is why you should study swimming pool and golf course facilities.

* Organisers should take alarm clocks, because it may be unwise to rely on local calls. Before a particularly important conference session it is worth booking an early morning call for everyone whether they like it or not.

* Know where the local hospital is and, if you are taking an important or large group to a slightly strange place, consider taking your own doctor.

* Introduce local gimmicks, such as getting everyone to wear a fez if you are in an appropriate country. It could relax people at dinner and even those who aren't over-amused will be careful to take them home for children.

* Take gifts from home for local helpers; don't inflict some of their own tourist souvenirs on them.

* It may not make much financial sense to take entertainers abroad. Use local entertainers when possible to liven a function, but vet them first.

* Take the trouble to learn a little about local customs, shaking hands etc., and remember that whilst it may be perfectly acceptable to mock or gently rib your own country, joking about a foreign one could cause offence.

* If locals are present at one of your functions, a company VIP should say at least a sentence or two in their language as a courtesy.

* Consider having visiting cards printed in both

your own and the local language.
* Make sure that post cards and stamps are easily obtainable.
* If it is a complicated venue, a plan of its layout and details of the services offered, printed in your own language, may be useful.
* Use company staff as workers rather than hiring local agency people. At least one good secretary will prove invaluable at an overseas function because there will usually be last-minute typing and organising; a bilingual one will be doubly valuable.

Problems at overseas venues

1 Assume that with the glamour of travel, sunshine and, probably, too much wine, there may be the odd drunk. Decide where to put them if they disrupt a function; the swimming pool would seem an appropriate place.
2 Decide how far you are prepared to put up with the inevitable moaner who will find something wrong with his room, his meal etc. Perhaps it's something to do with time zones but members of the travel trade will admit that there are those who, at their own expense, would happily holiday in a second-rate boarding house but will, when abroad at someone else's expense, find fault with a five-star hotel.
3 Brief the local police and consulate if your delegates are relatively high spirited; don't assume police practices are the same as our own.
4 It seems easier for people to make sexual fools of themselves when abroad, which can become embarrassing. It can also be frightening if it leads to blackmail, say behind the Iron Curtain. Most nightclubs would lose a lot of their appeal if delegates were forced to visit them in daylight but, failing this and assuming that some of your delegates will want to go nightclubbing, ask a reliable local to act as a guide.

7 Working with the venue

Booking

Before finally signing up a venue, whether at home or abroad, make one important check. Ask if any building work is planned around the time of your function. If you are booking a place out of season, that may be the time for remedial work. If there is even a hint of work planned, try to find somewhere else.

Then, before finally putting your booking in writing, consider the following details:

* Is there a hire charge purely for your function room? If so, haggle about it if you are bringing business to other sections of the hotel.
* What is the position over cancellation, or if your planned numbers fall?
* Be clear what is, or is not, included in the price you are quoted. What is the position over service and VAT?
* If there are personal bars in delegates' rooms,

    decide whether to have them emptied or, if
not, what arrangements to make for charging.
* How should extras be charged? Do they take
credit cards or cheques, and is there a safe for
valuables?
* If the venue charges for car parking, would a
voucher scheme be possible to avoid guests
having to pay? Failing anything else, consider
having someone standing by the cash desk at
the car park nodding guests through.

Once all the details are settled, put your booking in writing
and be quite clear on the terms. Your commitment under
the law will be just as firm as for any other legally binding
contract. For this reason, if you have been in negotiation
with other venues write to them spelling out that you are
not proceeding (this is courteous business practice of
course). It may be appropriate to make a provisional
booking to hold a date while you sort out other details, but
you must be clear when this booking has to be confirmed
otherwise you may cheerfully complete your planning
then find you've lost the venue.

Having settled the 'legal' side of booking the venue,
establish your working relationship with the place. The
hotel must know from whom they can take instructions
and both sides must be clear who is doing what; for
example, is the venue putting up the table plan or are you?

Check that no fire alarm practice is planned for the
middle of your function and that no generators or other
appliances are tested at various times. You need to know
where doctors and dentists are and whether the venue has
adequate first aid facilities.

When can you get in to set up and knock down any
display? Many venues will insist on a 'damage walk
through' after your function so that they can check if you
have left the place as you found it.

Other details? Will the hotel, or you, be able to coax the
local mayor along with his chain to a reception? Is it worth
telling the local press about your function? If nothing else,
it may get into the hotel's house magazine if it has one. Are
you going to put fruit and mineral waters in bedrooms

when delegates arrive? A nice touch if your budget will stand it because not everyone will want to rush to the bar as soon as possible. Are there small sewing kits, with shirt buttons etc., in the rooms, perhaps plus a hangover kit of aspirins? You may consider more elaborate gifts for VIP delegates. I wouldn't – functions should be used to break down distinctions between management levels, not increase them.

Decide if you will need to block off ugly areas in the function room, with flowers or display boards, and get a floor plan to help you in planning the layout for your function. It must be accurate because if there are pillars you will need to consider carefully any sightlines before finalising your seating.

Registration

Checking in at hotels

If possible, a quick handover system for room keys at hotels will avoid queues if delegates arrive together, say on a coach. If the hotel reception area is usually busy, consider a separate table set up in the foyer (with your logo above it) to handle quick registration for your guests. Take care with room allocations – feathers will get ruffled if a sensitive delegate feels that someone has a three-inch wider room.

Insist that the rooms you have booked will be ready when your guests check in. This is particularly critical in the middle of the day. If your delegates have to sit around on suitcases in the lobby, waiting for their rooms, when they are anxious to freshen up, they will not be over-impressed with your organisation. If necessary, you may have to book rooms for a previous night to ensure that they are ready for a mid-morning arrival; haggle over charges if it comes to this.

If and when the hotel staff go round turning down beds, make sure that the ritual does not fall at a time when all your delegates are showering or changing for an evening function.

Registering at conferences

Portable registration desks can be hired for conferences, or simple tables covered with green cloth laid out in an appropriate area may suffice. If there are numerous delegates, split them between check-in areas, either alphabetically (A–F, G–K, etc.) or by sales region or even by country; the respective areas for people to use must be clearly marked. Signs should be high up so that they can be read over people's heads. Interpreters should be available if there are foreign delegates. Distribution of badges should be slick. Either lay them out in alphabetical order or have a bank of assistants to type names straight onto badges at registration. Whatever system for registering delegates is adopted, it must not be officious. Be friendly and efficient because this will be the delegates' first exposure to your organising abilities.

Security

The degree of security for any function will depend on how confidential is the subject matter of your meeting, the country you are in and, sadly, on the current level of terrorist activity. For any function, 'security' must be an item on your checklist.

Gate-crashers

Having given thought to exactly who you want at your function, there may be those you don't want, industrial spies etc. Use people with tact in any registration area and on the doors; a fieldforce should be able to recognise trade delegates.

Tickets provide some security for large functions, although they are rarely asked for at dinners and they tend to be forgotten anyway.

If you need temporary staff in the UK, the Corps of Commissionaires (an independent non-profit making association) can supply ex-service personnel. They are smartly turned out with their badges of rank, cross belt and white gloves, and add a bit of tone but, like every other person involved, they need to be briefed properly. If you tell them to collect tickets but forget to mention that some guests may have forgotten theirs, then it is your fault if you find irate VIPs held up at the door.

VIPs

If any important public figures are attending your function, advise the local police. You may need additional hotel rooms for detectives/bodyguards.

Pilfering

Gifts for delegates should be put in their hotel rooms on arrival, if possible. If they have to be distributed during a meal, put them out at the last minute or hand them round towards the end of the meal, otherwise, sadly, hotel staff may steal them.

If there is expensive equipment on display, or in use, at your function then security guards should be hired over-night. As some display material may be highly combustible this security will also act as additional fire protection.

Bomb threats

Talk to the owners of the venue about their method of handling bomb threats and any evacuation procedure. At a large venue a code system may be used over the public address – some innocuous message like 'Will Mr Bellweather please come to reception' to indicate that a bomb threat has been received.

8 Travel

If delegates are travelling to your function in their own cars ensure that there is adequate parking and consider how their petrol expenses should be covered. Include a simple sketch map with your final instructions if the venue is at all difficult to find. If groups of delegates are arriving by certain trains then consider booking coaches to get them to the venue or, at the very least, an adequate supply of taxis – some stations have peak times when there are long queues.

If your venue is at all isolated, you may need to provide a coach shuttle between the hotel and the nearest town. If more than one venue is to be used, again, you will need a regular transport service between them. Such shuttles should run at regular times and to clearly defined places. Coaches should be air conditioned if possible and heated in winter (or cooled in summer) before delegates board and coach drivers must know exactly where venues are. Don't take it for granted that they will.

Tell passengers if it is safe to leave things on coaches, for example when getting off for a shopping trip or a factory tour. Point out interesting places to delegates on any journey. Coaches should be large enough to hold more than your party so that there is ample room, plus space for odd baggage. For smaller functions you could consider a vintage bus or horse-drawn coach as a gimmick which could get you coverage in the local press.

Travel abroad

Your function may be the first occasion abroad for some of your delegates and everyone, seasoned or not, will feel more at ease if they know exactly what is going on. Advise them in good time on the following points:

* What visas and injections are needed. Try not to make the list too off putting and if none is needed be sure to say so.
* Spell out insurance arrangements for luggage, medical treatment etc.
* Any special rules about cameras. Certain countries can still be difficult, while if you are revealing a product way ahead of public announcement, you may have your own rules.
* Duty free arrangements. Allow time in your schedule for shopping and advise delegates on the best places to visit. A conversion chart of continental and domestic sizes to help shopping for wives will be appreciated, while if there are wives along too it is worth persuading a local shop to open out of hours if it suits your timetable. One should be prepared to do so if the numbers are big enough.
* Tipping customs and any really unusual local customs (to avoid delegates giving offence).
* Times and places of local religious services.
* Whether a driving licence is necessary. If delegates will be driving, establish if their domestic licences will be accepted or whether international licences will be required.

* What sort of dress will be required. Women in particular will welcome this information. Think twice before asking men to take evening dress half way round the world for one gala dinner at which they may take off their jackets after the first course.
* Whether there is a swimming pool so that they can pack costumes.

Travel 'check list' cards are available which will be appreciated by delegates travelling abroad for the first time.

Finally, advise delegates not to forget their passports!

When they arrive and check into their rooms, delegates should find a welcome letter repeating some of the above points because they will have forgotten them.

Planes

Check the availability of aircraft seats at an early stage. They may be difficult to book at peak times (hotels may also be affected and too busy to cope with you adequately anyway). Even if you are chartering, a replacement plane may be difficult to find if one of yours breaks down at peak time.

A separate check-in desk for large groups at the departure airport will avoid queues and act as a gathering point. If you invite delegates for, say, a welcome cocktail party at a nearby hotel you may find that an airline will put in a special desk there if it is near to the airport. If you don't have such a function at a local hotel, at least see if you can gain access to your airline's executive lounge for your delegates.

Specify sensible reporting times, allowing for traffic delays, of course. However, delegates should not arrive too early (travel agents will tend to be unduly pessimistic) because this will get your function off to a dreary start. Remember that security checks add to boarding delays and will be hottest after recent incidents.

Be wary of booking some delegates first class, others steerage – class distinctions have no place on an overseas trip designed to boost company morale or team spirits, no matter what company 'rules' may say.

Airlines overbook, some by quite high percentages, so there is a possibility of a delegate getting bumped off a flight (usually on a last come, first bumped basis). You can get compensation but this will not be much help if a conference collapses as a result. Obviously it helps if yours is a big enough company to use some muscle, but any size of company should have a travel representative with them at this hour.

You must have a travel agency courier with you if you are taking more than just a handful of guests. Travel operators work on a rough average of one courier per fifty travellers, but you may care to increase this for a business function; you will be paying after all. Much will depend on the calibre and quality of ground staff used at the location by your agents.

Persuade the plane staff to welcome your group on board in their preamble. If chartering you will even be able to stipulate which film people see, but don't inflict a 45-minute technical film about your new chemical cracking process on them – poor timing.

Work out some simple system with the airline so that your guests don't have to pay for drinks and headsets during a long flight.

If you are flying in several groups, one after another, think of an emergency plan in case you get stuck with two groups at the same time because of bad weather or plane problems. If you are using a venue out of season, additional hotels may not be a problem but local transport may be. There should be at least one company host travelling with each plane load of delegates.

One final point on flying: don't put too many key company personnel on the same plane (to minimise the damage to the company in case of accident).

Ships

You could consider sailing people to an overseas venue but it might take a long time; at least you may be able to offer an alternative return trip by ship, perhaps partly at delegates' expense. One excellent use of a ship is as an hotel base for a tour of different islands as an incentive reward.

Luggage

Delegates will not relax properly unless they are confident that their luggage is being handled efficiently. You need the same confidence so, if possible, put someone in sole charge of baggage handling, finding porters, tipping etc. It will not be an easy job; it can take at least $1\frac{1}{2}$ hours to distribute luggage for 200 and some guests will start fretting long before then.

Despite the jokes about lunch in Frankfurt, dinner in Cairo, but luggage in Johannesburg, less than 1 per cent of cases actually gets lost. However, the jokes tend to make people edgy so set out your arrangements for luggage quite clearly in any final instructions to delegates. Ideally there should be specially printed luggage labels for your group (designed so that they can be folded over and used for both outward and inward journeys) or at least use a readily identifiable travel agent's label. Advise delegates to tear off old labels to avoid confusion. Many airlines, sensibly, will only accept luggage if it has the traveller's name and address on the outside.

If delegates are on a short trip, under-the-seat cases may save time in airports.

Money

You need to consider money for two groups: the organisers and the delegates.

Organisers need money to pay local suppliers, some of whom may insist on cash if your company has a reputation as a slow payer (word spreads around the travel world). You will also need enough to cope with emergencies. Transfer sufficient money to a local bank at your overseas venue or have a letter of credit. Gold plated credit cards are also helpful.

As far as delegates are concerned, the rule should be to spell out the rules. There may be exchange controls on how much money can be taken in and out of some countries. Warn delegates against breaking such laws and point out that in some countries, local under-the-counter currency exchanged could be counterfeit, with no comeback.

Advise people to log the numbers of travellers' cheques and, if possible, inform your delegates where it is best to change currency and if there is a delay. Incidentally, airports usually offer relatively poor rates of exchange.

Finally, it is worth advising delegates to carry only a small amount in cash for security reasons, although this will depend to some extent on just how villainous the local population is reputed to be.

Travel postscript

Whatever travel arrangements you make, set your schedule so that delegates have time to relax or see something of a country. Allow time for delays and don't, for example, put a key lecture or banquet at the start, because part of your audience may be missing. Even if they arrive on time, after travelling some way your guests may want to unwind before getting down to business.

One final tip: travel agents are not renowned for their familiarity with air fare structures, which can admittedly be complicated, and the commission system under which they operate does not encourage them to seek out the lowest fares. Get more than one quote.

9 Staffing and seating

The organiser

However carefully the many components of a function are considered, the success of the project will depend to a great extent on 'the organiser', the man or woman in charge of it all. Although the different components, travel, hotels etc., can be handled by different people, unless someone is in total control, and therefore able to stamp some authority and personality on the function, it may be less than 100 per cent successful. It should go without saying that the organiser must have full management trust and backing.

Support staff

The organiser, in turn, may need support staff either to arrange particular aspects of the function or to look after different groups of delegates. Where possible, support staff should be clearly identified either by badges or, for a major event, by clothing – blazers, flannels, ties, dresses etc. A uniform should be comprehensive. Suggest, for example, that everyone wears black shoes if appropriate; one helper in training shoes may kill the overall impact. If you decide on a uniform, you will need a company policy over who pays for what. If the event does not justify it, or your budget will not stand one, at least have some identification for staff, e.g. large name badges, ties, scarves or even T-shirts. It is important that delegates can readily identify whom to turn to for assistance. Different coloured scarves, ties or badges could perhaps be used to indicate different jobs and this should be explained to delegates in their briefing papers.

Serving staff and usherettes should be properly dressed, perhaps with an apron or overall that carries over the theme or colour of the function.

As well as support staff to work with delegates, the organiser may need one or more typists with access to a photocopier. At any function there may be last-minute changes which need explaining to people.

Incidentally, if meetings are to run over several days for different audiences, the ground staff should do the same jobs each day. It may be boring for them, but will lead to smoother organisation. Needless to say, all staff must be fully briefed.

The chairman

A key individual for a successful function is the senior company person present, whether it be the chairman, managing director etc. (for the purpose of this chapter, let us call him the chairman) because he is the one who can set the tone and make all the organiser's plans come to life. If the purpose of the function is to galvanise a fieldforce, the tone should be brisk and efficient; if the aim is to boost morale, the chairman may introduce a more friendly note. He should play a key part, and should not be used for trivia (e.g. to announce that car keys have been found). This should be a task for the organiser, who should also be the one to announce that 'the coaches are ready' etc. The organiser may delegate these jobs to a 'master of ceremonies' or to a toastmaster if one has been hired. Where possible the same person should make all such announcements so that delegates don't get confused by too many faces.

The chairman's main job will be to run the function and whether this means introducing a series of speakers or chairing a forum, he must clearly establish his control. Among other things the chairman should know the rules for running a meeting and he should have a proper gavel – too often meetings fall apart while people search for ashtrays or spoons to bang – and use it with confidence to get a function under way. He should introduce speakers with enough information so that delegates know who they are listening to, but should not go on too long or the speakers and the audience will become embarrassed.

During a questions session, either with a single speaker or with a panel, questions must be put through the chair; unless the chairman insists on this, the function may disintegrate into a series of fragmented meetings.

If acoustics are poor, or the audience has not heard a question, the chairman should repeat it without any shading; e.g. if the question includes a few sharp adjectives criticising the company, these must not be deleted by the chairman when repeating it. If a question is totally irrelevant the chairman should not put down the questioner but rather should offer to sort things out afterwards 'without taking up the time of the meeting now'. However, it is in order, and may be a popular move, to gently squash a smart Alec asking questions just to prove how worthy of promotion he is.

If written questions have been invited for speakers or panellists, the chairman should reserve the right to group them to avoid duplication and help the flow of things. An occasional summary will keep a meeting on track.

With a panel of three or four the chairman should get together with them before they go on stage to spell out exactly how he intends to run things. He should try to stop them squabbling too much (although a little controversy can add spice) and he should also suggest that they should not chatter indiscreetly before an open microphone.

Although the organiser at a dinner may be running things, the chairman should still keep an overall eye open and be on the alert for problems.

Seating at meetings and conferences

Much thought should be given to the seating arrangements, if a meeting or conference is to work well. The management at the venue should know how many a room will seat and in what formation, but you should still obtain an accurate floor plan and work out your own seating, if necessary using bits of paper cut to scale to represent lecterns, tables, chairs, etc. Watch pillars when planning seating because everyone must be able to see if they are to concentrate properly on your meeting and, if possible, don't put people facing windows or strong light as this can be distracting for listeners.

Boardroom-style seating will be most appropriate for small meetings, i.e. one large table with chairs around it. It is usual for the person at the head of the table to be in charge, so plan with that in mind. A classroom or school-room seating plan may be the best for a larger meeting if delegates have many papers or need to write. As the name implies, delegates sit at desks or tables, facing the stage or speaker. Theatre-style seating is perhaps the most common and enables more delegates to be seated than with other systems. There should be adequate gangways. Allow 0.9 square metres per person for a meeting or conference with seating in theatre style, 1.8 square metres per person if you are seating delegates in classroom formation.

Other points on seating for meetings and conferences are as follows:

* If someone is to speak from where he is sitting, for example at a meal, place him so that he will not have his back to anyone.
* People will persist in sitting near doors and at the back so, when you are loading a room,

ground staff should encourage people to
move to the front.

* Only the most feudal of us now leave seats
  free at the front for the squire; nevertheless
  seats should be reserved for any speakers or
  VIPs.
* Avoid speakers having a long walk when they
  have been introduced; it will kill the flow of
  the meeting.
* Take a head count to check if there are
  enough seats for people in the conference
  room or for a meal; if in any doubt, ask a few
  company staff not to sit down until all the
  guests are settled. If you are confident that
  there are enough seats for everyone at a meal,
  reserve places on each table at meals for
  company hosts.
* Allow latecomers into a meeting at appropriate points in the proceedings, not in the
  middle of an important lecture (the rustling
  and shuffling will distract others).
* At all costs avoid groups whispering to each
  other at the back of a room. If you have to give
  instructions to staff, go outside before doing
  so (having checked that the door does not
  squeak). One person muttering to someone
  else will take the edge off other people's
  concentration.

Splitting into groups

Delegates will usually want to sit with their friends,
although it may be advantageous to mix guests deliberately
so that, for example, traders or representatives from
different areas get to know each other better during their
time with you. Face-to-face meetings are only successful
with around a dozen or so and, if you have a large function,
you may consider splitting your delegates into groups to
discuss certain aspects of a subject, or their own problems,

in more detail. You can split by sales district, by alphabet, or simply by letting delegates sort themselves into groups, although this may take longer. Organisers have even had people going round singing songs until they identified the group singing the same song! If you do this at your function, allow a break of 24 hours afterwards while people get over the embarrassment of it all.

Perhaps the most efficient way to split delegates into groups is by giving them colour coded badges as they register. Plan the traffic flow with care when allocating groups to rooms. It is bad planning to have two groups trying to cross paths in a narrow corridor. If delegates must visit several rooms for different presentations, have a holding area because however carefully you plan, one speaker will over- or under-run and throw things awry.

Even if you split people into groups for most of their meetings, you should try to have at least one session with all the delegates together; this should be at the start or finish, preferably both.

Seating for dinners

The seating arrangements for a dinner, either in conjunction with a conference or as a separate event, can cause more work than almost any other aspect so, if possible, someone should be in sole charge of the table plan.

Round tables are perhaps better for a dinner than branches from a top table. A five-feet diameter table will seat eight people (avoid 13 at a table if you can). You need two feet width per person otherwise elbows will be bumping and branches from a top table need at least six feet between them for the serving staff to move about.

The best way to plan seating is to write guests' names on bits of card, shuffle them about on a floor plan, then shuffle them again. And again. And accept that you will still upset somebody.

Put a company man on each table as host and if there is more than one dinner during the conference, consider different seating plans at each one so that guests mingle. If there are after-dinner speakers, position their seating with care (for example, speaking across an empty dancefloor is not much fun) and don't put chief guests where they may become a butt for any cabaret artists you have booked. Sit your speakers in a logical order so that a microphone can be moved along without them getting too tangled up with wires.

Incidentally, get your timing right if you want an audience to 'clap in' the top table. Do not keep guests waiting too long while the mayor and managing director finish their sherry. It is discourteous.

10 Meetings

Small meetings, such as salesmen's get-togethers, form the bulk of business functions and are relatively uncomplicated to organise. As they are usually purely working sessions you will rarely be trying to impress anyone, although you should still choose a convenient and sensible venue and you should plan the working sessions so that no-one wastes any time. If delegates regularly attend such meetings it may make sense to use the same venue every time so that they get an idea of how long to allow to drive there; they may be able to slot in business calls on the way.

Annual general meetings

Company bosses are used to employees doffing their caps and may not be at ease in front of aggressive shareholders particularly with so many sensitive issues facing companies, e.g. race relations, sexual discrimination, consumerism etc. So the AGM may be looked on with some dread, but it must be faced and a company just has to swallow hard and organise one. Needless to say, the organisation should be impeccable; if you can't get microphones to work properly, shareholders won't think much of your business abilities.

The moral is 'be prepared'. If you have something to hide it is safe to assume that someone will find out about it and raise it in public. So, if you have bad news, get it out of the way fairly early in the meeting otherwise shareholders will be restless and won't be listening to your other points.

Some companies have considered splitting their AGMs into two, fulfilling their legal obligations as briefly as possible at one, with lower lights in the corporation facing inquisitors at another; understandable perhaps in view of the increasingly strident voices to be heard, but this does seem like an attempt to break the spirit, if not the letter, of the law. However, nothing says you can't spread company personnel about so that warm applause erupts throughout the room from time to time.

Tailor your venue and level of hospitality to how well you are doing. It is tactless to serve too much smoked salmon if you are forgoing a dividend. Conversely, don't sound too smug and complacent if you have good results to announce – shareholders may remember if you have depressing news in subsequent years.

Meetings with trade unions

Trade union meetings may have more impact on the success of a company than AGMs and should therefore be planned with as much care. Accepting that tempers may rise, choose a venue that can be kept reasonably cool and is quiet. Raising voices to overcome the noise of machinery may encourage heated emotions. Bear in mind that additional rooms may be needed to which the respective sides can withdraw during an adjournment.

Clear 'house rules' should be established for the conduct of the meetings so that there is no ambiguity and trust builds up on both sides. Proper records should be kept of what is said and a system should be developed for both sides to vet and agree minutes before they are circulated. It should be established whether any public statement is to be made after a meeting and it may of course be necessary to have a room available for the press. They may be less than sympathetic to a company if they have to door-step in the snow during prolonged wage negotiations for instance.

Employee presentations

Presentations to staff retiring, leaving or getting married need careful handling if they are not to be acutely embarrassing for all concerned. The worst thing of all is for the managing director to rush in and out because he is in the middle of an important meeting. This will be seen as gross discourtesy, particularly if someone is leaving after 40 years' service.

Whoever is arranging the presentation should establish well in advance who is to make the presentation and should also pick a convenient time of day to ensure a good turnout. People will expect in-jokes and someone should search through company files or talk to old colleagues in the case of retirements to dig out suitably scurrilous stories.

Finally, decide what is going to happen immediately after the presentation to fill the awful silence which usually follows.

Plant tours

If you arrange tours of any of your facilities for members of the public, the way you handle bookings says something about your organisation. Your system should be efficient and you should make any literature warm and friendly. Above all, give clear instructions on how to find a place and don't assume that everyone has a car; give tube, bus and train information. Teachers may welcome fact sheets in advance so that they can prepare pupils for the tour.

Above all, whether organising a plant tour for the public or for delegates to a conference, remember that people bore easily particularly if their feet are aching, and allow a break halfway through a long tour. Visitors will also get bored if they can't hear. A loudhailer or explanatory leaflets with numbers keyed to various work positions will be better than sending people away puzzled because they could not understand what was going on.

11 Conferences

If you plan an important conference with a dramatic sequence to announce a new product, consider having a simple card model of the arena made. Don't put the model on a coffee table and look down on it, because no-one else will; you must study it from eye level to give you an impression of sight lines. If you don't go to the expense of a model, an accurate floor plan is essential, plus side elevations to show sight lines to any screen.

However carefully you plan the room and sight lines, the key to the success of any conference is still the content. Plan the overall presentation before finalising each segment, otherwise the total effect may be disjointed. For example, decide in outline what various speakers are going to say before they write their individual contributions, to avoid duplication.

Information should be sorted into what delegates must know, what they should know and what it would be jolly nice for them to know but isn't really essential; if you grade information in this way you can easily decide what to leave out if you run short of time.

Having established an overall plan and the individual components, try to build 'bridges' between the presentations, such as the chairman saying: 'Well that was Fred talking about *A*, now closely linked with *A* is of course *B* so here is Charlie to talk about that'. It helps delegates to follow a theme if speakers cross-refer; too often conference presentations are delivered in less-than-splendid isolation.

Once individual contributions have been prepared, alter the running order if necessary so that something fairly light follows a heavy presentation. If something clearly becomes a major issue for the company as the conference planning proceeds, then make this a keynote address.

Don't crowd all your good points into the first session of a conference and avoid information overload. An audience won't absorb an endless stream of facts and slides. Remember that the subject matter may determine how much attention a speaker gets. 'How I seduced 50 famous film stars' will hold everyone, the latest position on current cost accounting may have less appeal.

In your planning, keep your audience in mind at all times, as well as the messages you are trying to put across. Don't make a presentation too lavish for the audience's needs. A relatively unimportant piece of information, instead of being padded out to fill an hour, may be delivered in 15 minutes and the rest of the hour spent discussing other business aspects. Avoid anything that will distract delegates, such as pretty girls holding up things (particularly their skirts) because this will break the concentration on your message. For the same reason, be wary of 'humorous sketches' to put across a message; if they backfire, the embarrassment can be painful.

Reveals

If your function involves the introduction of a new product to a fieldforce and trade outlets, you will need some way of making the announcement. The thought of thumping music, exotic dancers, smoke, or flashing lights, all to introduce a product which the audience has a vested interest in selling if it wants to prosper, may seem faintly ridiculous but, scoff though you may, adding an air of excitement to an announcement does seem to motivate people. However, any dramatic introduction of a product must be in harmony with the rest of the meeting; a long show sequence with an avant garde dance troupe would look unbalanced if the rest of the programme was a series of lectures given at an old blackboard.

Companies rarely have the in-house ability to put on a proper reveal sequence. But take care. Outside organisers may be too ambitious (after all, it's your money not theirs) and let a reveal sequence go on too long. (The more technically complicated it is, the more difficult it will be to shorten if rehearsals prove it to be tortuously long.) Remember that an 'over-the-top' reveal which becomes a parody of itself, may impress the dimmest 15 per cent of your audience, but will almost certainly offend the brightest 15 per cent. Which are the most important? Clearly, if you have an important product to launch, you should not just pull an old tablecloth off it at an appropriate point in the presentation. It is all a question of balance.

Rehearsals

You should have one or more rehearsals for your conference; even if there are only 12 delegates meeting in a small hotel with two head office staff, the latter should sort out who is going to draw the curtains, work the slide projector, shut off the telephones etc. Don't just muddle along as the meeting progresses because it will look, and be, inefficient.

For a large conference try to plan your rehearsals early enough for people to get at least some sleep before the Big Day (however carefully you plan, there are sure to be last minute panics). If rehearsals go on after midnight and things are still ragged, it helps if key speakers have understudies to read their golden words while the actual presenters get to bed. However, the organiser must work through the night if necessary otherwise the event may simply run out of time.

   Use a stop watch. It is important to know at the end of a rehearsal the exact length of each section. Allow for walk on/walk off times and, hopefully, applause. When you have timed it all, resist the temptation to make it any longer.

Other points

The success of a conference depends on attention to details like the following:

* A gala dinner as the highlight of a conference should have a separate organising team, or at least one individual in charge of it, because a dinner will need as much attention as the conference itself and, if it goes wrong, will be remembered long after.

* If there is a current sore point in the company, don't hold a conference and totally ignore it. One of the functions of a conference should be to act as a safety valve, so if there is a contentious topic, tackle it head on and get it out of the way; delegates won't concentrate on the rest of your message until you do.

* If important news breaks during your conference, announce it or put up a simple slide, don't let the information spread by whispers among your audience.

* Be wary of two-handed presentations. Duologues rarely work well unless both speakers are fluent and well rehearsed. Don't give each speaker a word or two to say each time, otherwise it will be a jerky presentation.

* Conferences need a little humour but this must not be laboured or over-rehearsed. I have seen a thunderflash and a satirically over-elaborate fanfare of trumpets played as the speaker was announced go down very well, but only because they were done with

impeccable timing. A comic slide of one of your key speakers taken, say, when a baby, may break the ice.

* Resist suggestions that top management should wear fancy dress or clown around, unless they are born comedians or recognised company 'characters'.

* If you hold a conference for one audience, say a sales force, then bring in another (such as trade customers) remember that you may need to rearrange your presentation. If so, allow time to rehearse the new words and tailor the scripts very carefully to suit the fresh audience.

* Do not play taped applause after a management speech; it will look odd if no-one's hands are moving. However there is nothing to stop you deliberately initiating a response by clearly signalling applause points. You will of course have company personnel primed to lead the applause, won't you?

Tell the local and trade press about any large conference, because it could make news. If you invite the press to your conference (and there are risks), there must be someone to look after them. Have a signing-in book so that you know who turns up. Make clear to journalists what is or is not on the record, but be realistic; don't attempt to embargo trivia because journalists will neither observe the embargo nor respect you for trying to impose it. Journalists should have a table near the front of the conference room and a separate room where they can work. They must be properly briefed and VIPs should be available to talk to them.

Incidentally, don't knock the competition in front of the press even if your comments are valid.

Press conferences

Although you may have only a handful of 'delegates' at a

press conference, the coverage may extend to a very wide audience so never treat such an event lightly. Above all, don't waste journalists' time if a press release would do just as well as your conference. (To some extent, your style will indicate the importance you place on your news and therefore tend to influence the coverage you are likely to receive.)

The arrangements for a press conference should be made with the same care as for any other meeting but, if anything, the participants should be extra carefully prepared. Here are a few points to remember:

* Company personnel should throw awkward questions at the nominated spokesman before the function. However, don't assume that all the journalists present will be similarly hostile, because it may lead the spokesman into being too aggressive and combative with journalists.

* A bright journalist may not ask pertinent questions in an open forum but may save them for later, so the spokesman should not relax immediately he comes off the podium; that may be when the journalist throws the difficult one.

* Don't tell journalists that you 'expect coverage'. You have no divine right.

* Having made a statement and invited questions, don't prolong the session. If 90 per cent of questions are gentle but the audience are running out of things to ask, a final, awkward one may blow up in your face by putting all the journalists on the attack.

* Management should be present rather than just PR staff, because journalists prefer to get at decision makers. If there is no alternative, have a telephone link with a key company VIP in another town or country. The VIP must be properly briefed and should always assume that the telephone is switched into the public address; it gets things off to a bad start if his

first words over an open line are 'Are the hacks ready for me?'.

* Have a signal for cutting off questions as a cue to the support staff that they should get the buffet ready and press handouts available.
* Time your press conference to hit the appropriate news deadlines.
* Don't hand out copies of speeches before a VIP speaks; it is insulting to read something which people are quite capable of reading themselves.
* Be quite clear what points you are trying to emphasise to the press.
* Keep your own staff informed; it is bad industrial relations for them to find out key facts from newspapers or television.
* Booze? Well, you need to know your audience. It is a bit tactless to serve expensive champagne if you are announcing redundancies to the press.

Exhibitions

Exhibitions and conferences will often be run together. If so, don't tack on an exhibition display without giving it careful thought. Define your objectives. Who are you trying to reach: old customers, staff or new customers? Why are you exhibiting? Too often the reason may be because rivals are taking space; perhaps you ought to have more positive reasons. The most positive reason is to sell so have a proper follow-up system afterwards and, if appropriate, brief the salesforce to bring key customers to the stand.

Calculate the true costs of an exhibition and try, difficult though it may be, to gauge its effectiveness. Are other exhibitions planned later in the year and, if so, can display material be re-used to cut costs?

If you are exhibiting in another country, see if you can get help (physical and financial) from government departments, e.g. trade missions, special shopping weeks, in-store promotions etc.

If you are exhibiting, all the points about venues mentioned in Chapter 4 should be studied, particularly concerning floor loading, access doors etc. Can your stand be seen from above when people are coming down stairs or escalators? If so, keep the roof in mind as a place for publicity material if the show regulations allow it.

Allow plenty of time for planning. That sounds obvious but note how chaotic most exhibitions are on press day at many trade shows. Thankfully, modular stands are becoming popular to keep down costs; money races to put up the most lavish stands often just profit stand builders. Modular display units will store easily and allow you to put on adequate shows without, perhaps, quite matching the effect of a purpose-built stand. Units must meet fire and safety regulations.

Two-tier stands, with perhaps offices or entertainment areas above, will need careful planning because the local authority will have a view on safety regulations and for all stands there may of course be height rules.

There should be a logical order to your exhibition and, if you are using it for different audiences on different days, vet the words on display. A huge mark up for your dealers may not impress some of your other audiences. Don't put too many words on display boards; people won't read them.

Finally, pay particular attention to staffing. Have a proper rota and make sure staff can be readily recognised, preferably by a uniform of some sort. If you have to bring in temporary staff, give them an adequate briefing on your company and the exhibits. If an exhibition lasts several days, company executives should not attend on the first day then forget all about it, otherwise the whole thing may become tacky by the end of the exhibition period.

12 Dinners and dances

Dinners and dances, though more social than meetings and conferences, may still have a part to play in your business affairs, e.g. as the highlight of a conference; if so, build up the event by calling it a gala dinner or banquet. If you've got the gall, you could call a fish-and-chip supper a gala dinner; it would sound better and no-one is likely to prosecute you under the Trade Descriptions Act. Mind you, there could be a keen sense of disappointment unless you handle it with great panache.

Obviously the choice of venue for a dinner is important and if possible should have a more elegant atmosphere than a room used for a working conference.

The guest list should be chosen with care; people may be more offended if they miss a dinner than other functions.

First impressions are vital, so send smart invitation cards with instructions on dress. The company chairman, managing director or other VIP and his wife should greet guests after they have deposited their coats and if a toast-master is announcing guests, don't let a long queue build up, otherwise they will get irritable.

Having been greeted, guests should preferably move into a cocktail party/drinks area for a half to three-quarters of an hour; this period should not be too long or guests may get drunk or restless. The programme should be even tighter if the meal is in the middle of a conference. If you overdo the food and drink, delegates will not concentrate after the meal.

Table decorations

As guests take their places for a meal they should be impressed with the atmosphere you have created in the room. A bold display of flowers can transform an otherwise dead corner and if you want to distinguish company officials on the day then a buttonhole may transform them too. It may seem strange to be discussing flowers in a book on business functions, but it does perhaps illustrate the degree of planning needed if your event is to be impeccable.

Hotels will quote for floral displays on tables but find out exactly what they are planning because, even for an all-male function, properly decorated tables can 'lift' the standard of your event. Someone in your organisation should be looking after such details.

When planning table displays, remember that holders are as important as the flowers; they must be stable and neatly presented because the most elegant flower display will be spoilt if a scruffy pot shows beneath it. Flowers should not be too delicate and wispy because they may have to stand for a few hours in heat and smoke; displays should not be too high otherwise they will prevent conversation across tables. Similarly, candles will stop eye contact and may even make a room too hot; if you use candelabra for initial effect, perhaps have them taken away after the first course.

Pay similar attention to other table decorations – book matches (ideally with your company or conference logo on them), streamers, menus, ashtrays etc.

If there are ladies at your function then a single orchid

each will be appreciated; they are available boxed with their own water container.

Graces and toasts

Consider a short thanksgiving before any fairly formal meal. There are no specific rules or regulations; it is entirely up to you so, if you wish, you can couple grace with good wishes to your delegates. Needless to say, it would be tasteless to couple grace with any promotional message no matter how bad sales are. In some organisations, it is customary for the chairman to introduce any top table guests at the beginning of a meal. Well, yes – but be brief.

Ask one of your senior guests to say grace and give him time to prepare; they may come up with something a little more original than 'For what we are about to receive'. The Selkirk grace, attributed to Robert Burns, can be moving if there is someone who can deliver it with the right accent:

> Some hae meat, and canna eat,
> And some wad eat that want it,
> But we hae meat and we can eat,
> And sae the Lord be thankit.

Nothing says that guests must stand to say grace although most will expect to do so; you should avoid guests bobbing up and down when they are really anxious to start their shrimp cocktails.

The next point during a meal at which guests rise to their feet may be for the loyal toast. This should be towards the end of the meal and should be given by the senior person present; glasses should obviously be filled. There is really no connection between the loyal toast and smoking although it is usual for the toastmaster to announce 'You now have your chairman's permission to smoke' immediately after the toast. If, as is increasingly likely, people are already smoking then either say nothing (to avoid embarrassment) or announce 'you have your chairman's permission to carry on smoking'. Some guests may wish to sing the national anthem or patriotic songs after the toasts; you can't stop them, though you may wish to hide under the table until they finish.

Other toasts? Well, some organisations have the chairman taking wine with certain groups, but this can jar at a business function. However, it is appropriate to invite the gathering to toast someone they all know who is, say, retiring after long and distinguished service.

Toastmasters

A red coat can certainly add class to a function and a toastmaster may help to control things by acting as a sheepdog to move guests in for a meal. He can also lead in the top table (if so, his gavel should be held high so that people can see where the crocodile is moving) and can handle tasks like getting serving staff out of the way before speeches start. He should also announce any 'comfort break' or whatever euphemistic phrase is used for a pause in the programme before speeches. A toastmaster should announce: 'The proceedings will start at such-and-such a time'; if he announces that the break is for twenty minutes you may have difficulty in getting the audience back.

The toastmaster will introduce any speakers. In theory, but rarely in practice, he should ask the chairman for permission to call on the speakers; at the very least he should check that everyone is ready before proceeding. He may later have to ask: 'May we have your respect for ...' if a speaker is having a rough time.

It is interesting to study a professional toastmaster in action; the better ones will even warn top table guests 'I'm going to bang behind you' before crashing their gavel down. Avoid chatty toastmasters who think that they are stars; they should be self-effacing. Bear in mind that they may not be relaxed enough to introduce a swinging cabaret, and remember that they will need to eat. For a function with a large number of guests, possibly scattered among several bars on arrival, two toastmasters may be necessary.

On balance, a good toastmaster will add something to

your dinner. However, some of them do stand on their dignity and may be pompous and try to run things their way. Take their advice of course, but don't stand any nonsense.

One area where a toastmaster should be able to help is how to address people in the introduction to a speech. As a broad rule, put guests in order of apparent importance. Anyway, you are unlikely to meet the widow of an Admiral of the Fleet very often and if you get things wrong the only person likely to notice is the one you put in the incorrect order. You can't win them all.

Divertissements

Small details may lift your dinner or banquet out of the ordinary.

* Consider piping in the beef as something of a ceremony; have drinks available so that the chairman can toast the piper. Pipers should not be asked to play for too long. People's threshold of boredom for Scottish tunes is quite low.
* Scots may wish to 'address the haggis', but this has to be done well to work. (On one occasion I saw a speaker fall drunkenly into the haggis half way through, which slightly spoilt the effect.)
* Gifts for ladies will be appreciated, as will free goodies of any kind. However high-minded we may be, guests like to take away bits and pieces, particularly things that their children or grandchildren can play with. If you load them with bits and pieces, consider giving them a carrier bag too, but do stop short of sending them away with an apple, orange and paper hat.
* Diversions such as a jokey sing-song with special words written to well known songs; or a mock version of some popular TV pro-

gramme, featuring a key guest, may go down
well. But don't let such things drag on too
long.

Prizegivings

If you are to present awards during your function, delegate
someone to look after this side and for heaven's sake get it
right; the state of the art is not well developed and presentations are often chaotic.

Collecting an award should be part of the joy of winning
it, but don't let a prizegiving become a marathon because
many guests won't know or care who has won what.
Develop a simple scheme so that you don't get the awards
muddled and, if there are trophies, make sure that the
bases don't fall off onto people's toes. If someone has won
more than one award present them all at once so as not to
involve them in several trips up and down the room.
Discourage prize-winners from making rambling 'thank
you' speeches.

Raffles

You may decide to run a tombola or raffle during your
function, perhaps as a fund raiser for charity. Guests like
the excitement of winning something during a dinner
dance and if it is purely for fun have plenty of small, fairly
frivolous prizes. As with a prizegiving, don't turn a raffle
draw into a great marathon otherwise guests will get bored.

A tombola might be better than a raffle because it can go
on throughout an evening and cause less disruption. But
do watch the law. It should be legal if the whole thing is
incidental to your main entertainment, if it all takes place
during your function (i.e. the selling of tickets as well as the
draw), and provided there are no money prizes and the
whole of the proceeds (less legitimate expenses) go for a
specific purpose. There have been suggestions that
drawing raffles in ascending order could be wrong because

someone winning, say, the third prize, has no chance of winning the first or second as his ticket is out of circulation. If in doubt, get professional advice.

Prizes for a tombola or raffle should be displayed for maximum effect. Several prizes of the same type, e.g. bottles, should not be placed together, but spread out. Clothing, such as T-shirts, should be opened out and books should be stood up not laid flat. If the display still looks tatty, put a bouquet of flowers in the middle and raffle that too. When a tombola or raffle display has been laid out, get rid of the boxes that the prizes arrived in. Keep the audience's age in mind when deciding on prizes.

Beware of auctions as fund-raising events. It can be embarrassing if two drunks bid each up to ludicrous amounts for a piece of trivia.

Music

A dinner dance will of course need music. If a band plays during a meal, to fill the silence, list the music on the menu if it is a formal function. A dance band should not tune-up during speeches. Tailor the music to the age of your guests; the top ten tunes of 10 weeks ago are probably a safe bet. If the bulk of your members are bulky, traditional music may be more appropriate. You probably won't want an aggressive or experimental group, although if your band are jazz specialists you could perhaps build in a fifteen-minute session by them as a cabaret spot during the evening.

Discos may be a better idea because at least the music won't be out of tune; a local radio station may co-operate and run a disco in return for some publicity. Pop groups, apart from the long-winded pantomime of setting up their equipment, will almost inevitably play too loudly for many guests. Conversely, military bands always seem to go well whatever the age of an audience.

When you come to dancing, dim the lights and suggest to a few company personnel present that they should take the floor first if things seem slow. Consider whether you

should have spot prizes and, later in the evening, a cabaret.
Steer clear of audience participation shows – not everyone
enjoys them.

Remember the following final thoughts on dinners and
dances:

* Remove microphones before photographs
  are taken of top table guests.
* Serve coffee at the dinner table not in a
  lounge outside.
* Clear tables before speeches start, otherwise
  your costs may go up because long-winded
  speakers will put the staff on overtime.
* Some hotels may encourage you to leave a
  room while it is cleared for dancing (this may
  partly be to help increase their bar sales).
  Avoid this if you can because it disrupts the
  flow of the event.
* If you have to rearrange the room for dancing
  after a meal, work out in advance how the
  tables will then be placed.

13 Food and drink

Food

While you are busy feeding your delegates' minds with your messages, don't forget to feed their stomachs. If you neglect this side you will mar the impact of your function. If your event is to be at a company location your own caterers, given time, will almost certainly rise to the challenge of supplying appropriate refreshments, but don't expect other venues to cater out of their class; they are unlikely to be able to do so. If you are using a venue which does not normally handle catering then if possible during rehearsals put your ground staff (if you have enough of them) through the exact meal that your delegates will eat as a test run.

Having settled on your venue, sit down with the manager and chef and plan your food requirements. The age and style of your audience will, to some extent, dictate your needs. The young eat more than the old; women eat less than men; a sophisticated international audience will accept foreign food, others will be put off. If in doubt, don't be too bold or way-out in your choice of food.

The time available for a meal will affect your planning. If there is only limited time for a meal, say in the middle of a conference, don't be so ambitious with the menu that delegates have to rush back for the afternoon session. Small details count; for example, ice cream and chocolate sauce will take longer to serve than trifle.

You will know from your audience whether you need to offer vegetarian or kosher food. All this is very much fine tuning, of course, because presumably minority groups who attend functions do so for other than gastronomic reasons. Some hoteliers always have cheese and fresh fruit salad available, which seem to suit most tastes, but if you have a specific ethnic group to cater for make special arrangements as a courtesy.

Crisps and biscuits

These are ideal scattered around in dishes on tables if people just want a snack; they must be fresh and supplies must be topped up regularly. Try to be a little different and provide something other than plain crisps; if special biscuits are made locally, then serve them. In addition, mints can be put on the table in a function room.

'Airline' meals

If time and catering space is limited, ready boxed 'airline' meals (complete with cutlery and a bottle of wine) can be an acceptable substitute for a more formal meal. There must be space, even if only stairs to sit on, to eat the meal and a slick method for clearing away the boxed debris which will not be a pretty sight.

Wine and cheese

Wine and cheese make cheap and informal refreshments but do get good cheese, and offer celery with it. Provide out-of-the-ordinary cheese biscuits to show that you have used your imagination and make sure they are fresh. Put up posters explaining the various cheeses, if appropriate to the occasion.

Barbecues

Barbecues will rarely be fitting for a business function unless you have the right venue and want to introduce a degree of informality. The organiser must know what he is doing and have barbecue experience; a line of people waiting for potatoes whilst someone tries to get a fire going will not leave a very good impression. Remember that lanterns and fires attract insects; have plenty of bins for litter and, to be on the safe side, have a first aid kit and fire extinguishers available.

Breakfasts

Breakfast functions, although unpopular with some, can work if you are convinced that your audience will be prepared to get out of bed in time. The results must be worth their effort so use your imagination with the menu and the programme for the meeting. They will not be popular after late nights.

Buffets

Buffets are not necessarily cheaper than a formal meal. It is not easy for hoteliers to maintain portion control and an attractive buffet may encourage guests to eat more than they would at a normal sit-down meal. The advantage with a buffet is that people can mingle.

Don't put the food and the bar by the doors or there will be congestion; a buffet must flow so that as guests move along the serving table their meal gradually builds up. Choose the food with care; avoid things which need cutting and don't expect applause after a speech if guests are holding a drink in one hand and a plate in the other. Don't leave food out too long in a hot, smoky room; have the plates covered to keep it fresh. Seats should be available for the old, handicapped or tired.

Dinners and banquets

These need careful planning because, as they are more formal, guests will have higher expectations. The real test for an organiser is a full-scale sit down dinner or banquet (only the degree of lavishness really differentiates the two).

The most important thing with a sit down meal is that the organiser, hotel management and chef are in sympathy; not sympathising with each other over a disaster, but in tune with what the organiser is trying to achieve.

Be realistic. If there are 800 guests at your dinner, no hotel in the world will be able to serve a meal as appetising as it could to the same number over a phased booking schedule; it is unreasonable even to expect it. An hotel and its staff will do their best if you work closely with them, and that includes setting a clear start time and trying to stick to it. Casseroles or cold dishes present no problems if you are late, but not so roasts; if the chef has cooked duck, it may be superb after two hours but ruined after two-and-a-half; the same with beef.

Discuss with the chef his specialities, but don't push your (or your chef's) luck by deciding on soufflés, omelettes, zabaglione or beef wellington; they can be too risky. Avoid choosing any dish which it is reasonable for diners to be asked how they would like it cooked. The serving staff won't have time to go around asking how people like their steaks done.

If in doubt, stick to fairly well known dishes and don't get too neurotic about fresh rather than frozen vegetables. Not many people will tell the difference.

Vary the course to add variety to a meal – a light then heavy course, then light, etc. Sorbet is a cheap extra course and gives the palate a break between two heavy courses. Try to vary the colour of your food; your delegates may not notice that you have considered this, but they may if the same coloured courses are served up one after another (leeks have a singularly unfortunate appearance and a very poor colour).

Research shows that the most popular meal in Britain is tomato soup, steak and chips followed by gateau. So now you know what to avoid! Be more imaginative; smoked mackerel makes a nice starter and corn on the cob is growing in popularity but can be rather messy to eat. If you are looking for a relatively cheap but good meal, steak and kidney pie, well presented, can be fine. Consider serving cheese before a sweet; this will have the advantage of letting guests carry on with red wine if the cheese follows a meat course.

Have a rough idea of the serving times of various courses so that you can keep to your timetable as the meal progresses. Much will depend on the chef (a great artist may be temperamental), the layout of the kitchen and the ratio of serving staff to guests. It helps if your first course is cold and ready laid out. Hors d'oeuvre makes a nice starter but is slow to serve if guests are given the opportunity to pick and choose.

If your budget will allow, petit fours or mints with the coffee can make the difference between a memorable or mundane meal at very little extra cost and give diners something to eat as they put a sugar substitute in their coffee.

Cigars? I'm not sure why non-smokers should subsidise the others, but cigars may be expected at the end of a formal meal.

Drink

Coffee

Coffee is the most consumed beverage and the worst made; standards vary enormously. Poor coffee is often due to the wrong beans being used in a machine; if caterers would only follow manufacturers' instructions for using equipment perhaps standards would be higher.

Test the offering at your venue before your function, complain vigorously if it is bitter, and ask them to use high quality coffee in newly opened packs.

Having approved the standard of coffee, make sure that supplies are adequate. You may need copious cups for workers putting presentations together late at night. On the day, be sure that you have coffee available ahead of your scheduled start time because some delegates are bound to be early.

Take care with Turkish coffee; it can go sadly wrong and be offputting, while Gaelic and other coffees are tempting but can take too long to serve in any quantity.

For a dinner dance, consider serving coffee or soup towards the end of the evening.

Tea

The standard is slightly higher with tea than coffee, though not much. Offer lemon as well as normal tea, but don't experiment with unusual blends which may not be to everyone's taste.

The key with both tea and coffee at any break in a function is to get the timing right so that the drink is ready and hot; if a speaker is badly over-running then warn the caterers. If in doubt, it should be available early. If possible, cue the serving staff so that some cups can be filled ready as delegates tumble out of the meeting room.

Water

During a meeting, clean fresh water should be available on all tables where delegates are seated boardroom or classroom style; carafes look better than jugs and leave less landing room for flies, while squash and mineral waters make refreshing touches. Liquids provided for speakers should be cool but not over-iced because the cold could affect the vocal chords.

Alcohol

There is ample scope for fiddling with alcoholic drinks so be very clear what you are paying for when negotiating with a venue. Perhaps ask someone from your own catering department to monitor what is going on. It may be possible at some functions to have alcoholic drinks on a sale-or-return basis. Serving staff should know if drinks are included in the cost, as should guests. It has been known for staff to try to charge for drinks that are in fact on the house. There is always confusion as to what happens to full or half-empty bottles left at the end of a banquet; increasingly people are seen taking them away.

The supply of drinks is one area where it is easy to be seen to be mean. If you cut off supply just as a party is going well, people may remember that rather than the message of your function.

If the drinks are at your expense, consider putting out beer and squash at the end of a meal when dancing starts, leaving guests to buy more expensive drinks themselves.

At cocktail parties or buffets don't serve drinks which are too strong. It could be dangerous particularly if you are serving an unknown punch and people are driving. Guests will drink more when it is free, but there will be less consumed per head if women are present. Consider cocktails as a gimmick, perhaps in half pineapples, but only serve a limited selection otherwise service will be slow.

You must have professionals to serve drinks; ensure that they are not likely to run out of ice and lemon. One section of the bar should be for waiters only, otherwise people sitting around will wait for ever. Drinks taken round on trays will ease the strain on a crush bar.

Liqueurs? If your budget will stand it they should certainly be offered at the end of a meal.

When serving alcoholic drinks, check any licensing laws; if it is a non-licensed venue get advice or co-operation from a local licensee. Be sure that you are within the law. It will be bad publicity if the police raid your function as guests are singing Auld Lang Syne.

Wine

If you are choosing and paying for the wine, it should obviously match the food served. If not inclusive, the ordering system for guests must be simple, perhaps with a clearly signed desk in the cocktail area; staff must not be allowed to collect cash during any speeches.

Don't forget wine for the top table; you will get around six glasses per bottle and consumption is approximately four drinks per hour per head. If you are on a tight budget, tell the serving staff to say 'this is for the toasts' as they serve the last glass.

Wine should not be forced on guests; the staff should ask before pouring second and third glasses. Remember the following points:

* Many women prefer sweeter wines than men.
* Rosé wine is rarely served, which seems a pity.
* The chairman may be invited to taste one of the bottles of wine, although this is something of an irrelevance (I can't think what the average venue would do if the wine was rejected).
* White wine is better chilled, red should be at room temperature.
* If you are in an area which has its own wine then serve that as a novelty.
* It is a waste of money to serve expensive wines to the average audience; the only people you will be impressing are yourselves. Few people know very much about wine and, as consumer tests show, supermarket wines are perfectly good enough for most functions. Certainly the house wines or one recommended by the hotel manager should be adequate for your function. Try it first of course.
* If you are serving hot and/or spicy foods, the choice of wine will be even less critical.
* As gentle interludes in a programme, wine tastings can be good fun and very revealing.
* Don't use saucer glasses for champagne. The ubiquitous Paris glasses are perfectly adequate.
* Never serve homemade wines, even if wine-making is the chairman's hobby.

Serving staff

If you have paid an anonymous visit to vet your venue, you will have some idea of the calibre of the serving staff and whether it needs reinforcing. You need one waiter per eight to ten people at a dinner to serve food; one per twenty-five guests for wine, with a slightly higher ratio for top tables.

Staff should be properly informed about your function – hearing a good head waiter briefing banqueting staff will bring back happy memories for servicemen – and they should also know what any unusual course is because someone is bound to ask them.

During your function the staff must know from whom they can take orders and you, as the organiser, must know who to liaise with at the venue.

Waiters with furthest to go should head the queues in the kitchens, although not to the extent that the top table is drinking coffee while other guests are still waiting for their main course. It is quicker and involves less mess if waitresses serve vegetables rather than have 'family service' where dishes are put on tables and guests serve themselves. Unless service is very stretched, never place full plates of ready laid out food in front of guests; aim for a little more elegance.

Other serving points to be remembered:

* Guests should be offered a second bread roll during a meal.
* If you want to air your knowledge of the catering world, stress that you want 'crumbing down' to take place (clearing tables of the debris from bread rolls) before later courses are served.
* Plates should be hot when appropriate.

Finally, whether at a coffee session or full banquet, dirty cups and glasses should be cleared away as soon as possible. On a safety note, remember that broken glass can be dangerous and should be removed quickly.

14 Speaking

No matter how much attention is paid to your venue, food and slide sequences, the words spoken are the key to the success of any function. This chapter is aimed at speakers and lecturers, and the organiser (who may also have to get on his feet from time to time) may care to, tactfully, show this section of the book to his performers.

The same rules apply whether you are making a speech, delivering a lecture or just 'saying a few words' at a cocktail party and the first rule is that you can't lay down hard and fast rules. The innate ability to speak varies with each individual; outstanding speakers are born not made although it is possible to make some improvements to almost any speaker. This is not the place to consider such detail as elaborate breathing exercises (I don't believe in them anyway), but companies could consider outside speaking courses for executives (standards among them vary enormously) or organising one in-house. Improvements can result from simply asking people to prepare two- or three-minute speeches, video recording them, then playing them back so that speakers can see themselves in action.

Preparation

The biggest problem a novice public speaker may face when he is first asked to perform is nerves. These will be less if it is simply a case of reading a presentation with slides, but nerves should not put people off as they can be contained. If you, as an organiser, want a particular person to speak, coax them into firmly committing themselves before you mention that there will be 850 people in the audience.

Nervous tension is a normal reaction with any strong emotion and you can't do very much to control it, although experience helps. Nerves are a throw-back to uncivilised life thousands of years ago when meeting an adversary meant maximum muscular effort, either in flight or fight. (Some speakers I've heard wouldn't have to be thrown back very far.) Adrenalin stimulates various glands and organs and the heart rate increases; blood pressure rises; 'fuel' in the form of glucose is mobilised from the liver storage and sweat glands in the skin increase output to carry away the excess heat to be produced. In other words, all is made ready for you to perform at maximum efficiency. This is all very well for athletes and other sportsmen, but the only part you will be using when speaking is your brain and all that chemical chaos in your body may cloud your thought process. Relax – once you are on your feet the tension will almost certainly vanish. However, if you are a chairman or MC at a function, remember that some of your speakers may be nervous and do what you can to calm them; at a function do not insist on chattering too much to a speaker next to you if he is clearly engrossed in his notes.

Before preparing a speech or lecture, you need to ask:

*   What is the audience? What size? You may
     need different approaches for small and large
     groups.

* What is the audience expecting of you, what message etc.?
* How long are you supposed to speak? If it is a wide subject, ask for a specific brief. Remember your delegates won't take in too much information.
* Who else is speaking? In what order are speakers performing? If several speakers are appearing at a function, it must be planned so that there is no duplication, which means liaising before detailed preparation work is done.

Having answered those questions (and others which may be appropriate just to you) remember that content is vital; you won't be too audible if you talk through your hat. Although set speeches should be planned well in advance, especially if there are visuals to be prepared, remember that information is a perishable commodity and as it gets old it may get dangerous. Conference speeches should be bang up to date; delegates won't thank you if they travel a long way to listen to rehashed old news. Preparing speeches in advance has another danger; senior management may want to vet them and if one thing is certain, it is that speeches written and re-written by committees are unlikely to motivate anyone; the closer to the day a speech is prepared, the less time there will be for interference.

A speech must be in tune with an audience. You may be deeply interested in a subject but don't assume everyone is.

When preparing a speech or lecture, jot down the main headings that you want to cover, then list under each one the various points you hope to put across. Sort these into a logical order, then run through the headings and points again to see if they have a natural flow and make sense. Rearrange the order if necessary and don't be afraid to delete things. If there is one fundamental fault in all talks, it is that they are too long.

Rather than write out a speech, talk it into a tape recorder then have it typed; it may be more natural because it will have been said rather than written. Emphasis on correct grammar seems less critical nowadays so you need not use too formal phrasing; the important thing is to be understood.

Speaking manuals stress the importance of a good introduction. There is some merit in this, but don't devote a lot of time to a superb introduction then follow it with a poor speech. Your audience will simply have a bigger let down.

The style of a speech should be uniform. If it is an erudite, witty speech then a crude, earthy section with four letter words will simply dismay listeners.

As you proceed through a speech, include signposts between sections, for example: 'So that's X, now let us consider for a moment Y'. This will help to carry an audience with you.

Phrases and words should be short and simple; dispatch means send, so say send. 'At this point in time' means now, so say it. The meaning of a word or phrase is not what you think it is, but what your audience understands it to be.

A talk should not be too bland. Don't be afraid to argue with yourself; for example: 'You may say that. . . .' and then put a counter-argument (taking care to demolish it). Beware of too much of 'on the other hand, on the other hand. . .' otherwise your audience will feel that you have no positive views.

Above all, be sincere, and that means using your own voice. A dialect is fine, provided the audience doesn't need an interpreter to understand you. And being sincere means not using over-elaborate praise; if you laud someone to the skies it may just sound silly.

Roget's Thesaurus is useful when preparing speeches and lectures, as are a few good books of quotations. Use words to paint pictures. For example, if you are describing a new warehouse, give the size in square metres, but also say how many football pitches that represents.

Beware of jargon and abbreviations. The European Community is littered with various abbreviations for organisations but not all your audience will understand them, nor will all of them understand foreign phrases. Beware of saying 'For example', then wandering off and losing the thread of your talk in the process.

When speaking to an outside audience, don't over-praise your own company. When you have prepared your golden words, go through and delete the excess super-latives and clichés (some speeches could almost consist of a series of cliché cards which are shuffled into order then duly read).

Using notes

At some point you need to decide whether you are a speaker (using brief notes or even ad libbing) or a reader, ploughing through prepared pages of paper, word by word. If you are nervous, and have a lot of slides, then write it all out and read it; use big type if you wear glasses – better than fiddling with bifocals. At least the content will be accurate and you will have a good idea of how long it will take. Remember if you are reading a presentation not to put 'it is raining' but 'it's raining'; insist on the typist abbreviating like this otherwise your talk will sound stilted.

A talk is better if it is not read, because even with invisible prompters it is obvious that you are reading something. Should you learn a speech by heart? I'm not convinced. It can be very hard work and a speech can sometimes be slightly wooden because an audience can almost 'see' the speaking looking ahead in his mind to the next word. If you do decide to learn it by heart, have a copy of it in your pocket in case you dry up on the day.

If you know your subject well, have spoken about it several times and can ad lib with confidence that is a better method than memorising it word for word. The result will sound much more convincing.

However, for the average speaker, using bullet point notes may be the most effective system because it can make a speech sound lively. Make your notes on fairly stiff card, say the thickness of a postcard. Most speakers seem to use a series of postcards with string through the top left hand corner but if your speech isn't a very long one, consider putting all your notes onto one piece of card which, when folded, will slip inside a breast pocket. The advantage with a card like this is that if you drop it, your notes cannot get out of order.

If you use conventional note cards, don't have so many that you look as if you are doing card tricks and, whatever sort you use, space your notes out so that there is room to modify them as you approach the delivery of your speech.

When speaking at an outside function and there are one or two questions still to be resolved (e.g. is it a council or a committee) pencil these queries on the top of your first sheet of notes and get them answered before you speak.

Vital items should be marked in your notes with a magic marker. Conversely, points that are not particularly critical may be put in brackets and omitted if the audience seems fairly uninterested.

When speaking to foreigners, at least attempt something in their language; write it out in your own language, get it translated and then persuade a native to tape-record it. Using phonetic notes, have it re-typed in whatever gibberish you like as long as, when you say it, it sounds like the foreign tongue.

Visual aids are dealt with in detail in Chapter 16 but, if you are using them, get together with the operator and sort out who is going to press the buttons. If it all goes wrong, you will be the one with egg on your face. Know what slides are going to be on the screen at any point, by having a description or reproduction of them in your notes. Pause as a new slide comes up, because at that moment the audience will be concentrating on the screen, not on you.

Although you can get different types of pointers (from billiard cues to light beams) beware of them in general. If you have notes and an audience to contend with, you don't want to be playing with a pointer at the same time. It can be argued that if you need to point to something on a slide, then the slide is not sufficiently clear in the first place. If you have a binder with a script for slides in it, it could be worth having a second copy of the script at the back, doctored so that it needs no slides; you could then turn to that if anything goes wrong with the projector or other visual aids.

Humour

When people laugh they take in oxygen which keeps them awake, but there are more problems over humour in speeches and lectures than in anything else. The worst words in any speech are 'That reminds me of the story of...' followed by a long rambling tale which reminds the audience of absolutely nothing. If one thing in this book should be written in capital letters it is this: YOU DO NOT HAVE TO TELL JOKES IN A SPEECH OR LECTURE.

You will be more nervous, or you should be, if you are telling jokes because you are more at risk and if you are not a natural story teller, don't. In fact, humour needs more 'don'ts' than 'dos'. After-dinner speaking may be rather like up-market music hall, but don't tell racial or blue jokes; don't use in-jokes which few will understand; don't tell a string of jokes one after another (this does not count as a speech); don't try long complicated jokes, the agony lasts longer if you go wrong; don't do impressions unless you are very sure of yourself; don't plough straight into another joke if one flops, give up instead. Don't signal that something is supposed to be funny. Although it sounds obvious, don't put the punchline of a joke first – speakers often do.

Having given those awful warnings, do try to lighten your speech with wit. That's where the books of quotations will be useful. Referring to something that has happened during the function will usually bring a smile; references to escape parties at conferences are popular. Remember that men take ribbing better than women – honestly – but be careful that you don't slander someone.

Finally, resist the temptation to pun; the groan from the audience will only just be in sympathy with you.

Rehearsing

You should deliver your speech to yourself a few times so that you are totally familiar with it and do not stumble over key phrases 'on the night'. You could try taping it, which may at least cure you of mannerisms like 'you know' etc. It has been suggested that you should deliver a speech into a tape recorder in front of a mirror but this can be very artificial, so don't take too much notice of the result. A better way is to deliver your speech to a friend, who is new to the subject, to see if he gets the messages that you are trying to put across.

Just before speaking

To some extent you are 'on stage' when addressing an audience, so over- rather than under-dress but don't clutter yourself with flashy jewellery or anything which will distract. Dress is critical; women as an audience may be watching this point with keen interest but, again, too much jewellery may make you look like a fortune-teller about to start reading palms.

Allow plenty of time when arriving at a venue; it is better to be half an hour early (perhaps sitting outside in your car rather than in a smoky room) than five minutes late. Arrive in time to try the microphone and the height of any lectern; this is crucial if you wear glasses. If it is a smoky room, nip outside for some fresh air before speaking, telling the organiser where you are going, and go to the toilet. If you disappear at the end of the dinner to do this, tell your neighour how you like your coffee if it has not yet been served.

If you are staying at the venue where you are speaking, consider returning to your room to clean your teeth and generally freshen up, and if during the meal you are nervous and your neighbour keeps nattering, gently ask him if he would leave you alone to concentrate on your notes.

Avoid too much, if any, drink before you speak; a microphone will pick up the slightest slurring in your words and you should not mix drugs (e.g. tablets for hay-fever) with drink. A glass of water should be available because your mouth may dry up with nerves.

Although you will be concentrating on your own

address, listen to other speakers, particularly if you have not heard them before. They may cover some of the points you propose to make. Polish up your speech as the event goes on. If there is hostility to a point made by a previous speaker you may need to address it before you go into your main theme, rearranging your order if necessary. Join in the applause for other speakers; it will help to warm up the audience for you. Be sure that the coffee service has finished and staff have departed before you start to speak; you don't want any distractions.

If you are speaking at a dinner and the audience has long lost interest, perhaps because it wants to get on with the dancing, then cut your speech. If the date changes on your watch during a function before you speak, you should certainly cut it. The key to good speaking is to know when to say nothing, which means cutting long and complicated anecdotes.

It is easy to misjudge an audience; months ahead, as you sit in your office and plan your speech, they will seem sober and intelligent. At 23.30 after a good meal they may not want a speaker pontificating on global markets for fertilisers.

If you are a supporting speaker and the audience is really waiting for a heavily billed star, don't drone on otherwise they'll become impatient. However, don't apologise for the fact that you lack speaking experience. With luck, they won't notice.

Finally, before you get to your feet, empty your pockets of anything that is likely to jangle, bulge or distract.

On your feet

As you are introduced, push your chair back, push any crockery out of the way in front of you, take a deep breath, then switch on and concentrate.

Take a little time at the start in order to gain attention and, if you are totally unknown, perhaps begin with something of a shock in order to grab interest.

Be enthusiastic. Use your normal voice and don't try to alter the pitch or you may squeak; if you use a false voice you may drop your aitches at a critical point which will sound worse than dropping them throughout. You may have to pitch your voice higher to fill a big room, but don't overact or orate – it will sound silly.

Try to have eye contact with your audience but don't pick on one person and stare at him throughout your speech, it will embarrass him. Don't put your key message in too early; get their confidence first. The only exception is if you want the press to take away a particular point – you may have to build it in early so that they can file their story in time for press deadlines.

Think on your feet. As you gain experience, it should be possible for you to modify (in other words, most probably, cut) a speech while you are delivering it.

Irritating mannerisms will not matter too much if you have great charisma, but remember the following points:

* Don't fiddle with watch straps, notes or spectacles.
* Don't be furtive when using notes; it could look as if you are studying pornography. (You may find yourself doing just that if using prompting aids; mischievous operators have been known to relieve boring sections by putting nude pictures into the system. Some speakers have all the luck.)
* Don't bang on a table or microphone.
* Don't turn away from an audience too long, for example if you are using a board of some sort.
* Don't put your main verb at the end of a long sentence; the audience may lose your thread.
* Verbal mannerisms are as annoying as physical ones. Such horrors as 'er, I mean, like, actually, in fact' all slip into speeches and sound terrible, you know.

If you are speaking on a highly charged subject and there is one section which may be quoted, get it right. Don't hesitate to look down at notes and read it accurately. If you are reading a speech all the way through, it is worth putting in an occasional section where you look up, away from your notes, and ad lib on a particular point. Don't get so carried away that you have re-entry problems back to your main theme. If you lose your thread or drop a clanger (and the chill in the room will be awful because people will be embarrassed for you) try to carry on. I have sat through many hundreds of speeches and never heard anyone dry up totally.

Signal when you are coming to the end with a phrase like 'and finally' but, having said that, don't drone on for another half hour.

You may have to deal with hecklers. Rabble-rousers on television newsreels have encouraged the lowering of standards at functions, although if you are pompous you deserve to be heckled. It has been said that at every lecture there should be someone at the back of the hall shouting 'poppycock'. It may be a bit mean to heckle guest speakers but it often seems to happen. A persistent heckler may help you because he will put the audience's sympathy on your side. Don't leave yourself wide open with rhetorical questions. If you say 'I expect you are waiting for me to sit down'; well of course they are and somebody may say so. If as an introduction to your views on how to solve a problem in your industry, you cry 'What is the biggest problem facing us today?' someone may well shout 'the beer's flat'; the roar of laughter will kill any serious intent you may have had.

Here are a few final thoughts on speaking:

* Passing something among an audience to examine is slightly dangerous because you may lose attention.
* When you have finished your speech, put a cross or tick against anything which went badly or well so that you remember it next time.
* In any talk or presentation, timing is critical, as is the way you deliver your speech. Don't sound too glib and slick; don't be pompous; don't gush; don't fall in love with the sound of your own voice; don't shout at an old

audience (they won't all be deaf) and don't talk down to the young.

* After all those 'don'ts' one 'do'. Do use pauses, particularly if you have emphasised an important point. A pause to give people time to reflect is fine, although one which makes the audience think you have lost your place is simply disconcerting. Don't leave obvious pauses for applause; it is conceited and you will be embarrassed if there isn't any. If you get a reaction (either laughter or applause) stop, wait for it to die down, then pick up the thread again. Don't laugh at your own jokes.

15 Sound and light

No matter how carefully you select your venue and speakers, your function will not succeed unless the audience can see and hear properly, so these aspects must be given close attention. Lighting, if handled properly, can add atmosphere and help to lift an otherwise drab venue.

First check the acoustics, because these will dictate what sound equipment you may need; poor acoustics may be improved by the careful placing of screens.

You will want the audience to concentrate on the golden words of your speakers so the room must be quiet. Block off, or preferably remove, any telephones and disconnect public address systems. Never rely on an operator's promise not to broadcast during your meeting; shifts change and a new operator may not be briefed. Neglect this and you can be certain that just as your meeting reaches a climax, a nasal message will boom out asking Mr Jones to report to reception.

Keep noise out; if your projection equipment is noisy it should be housed in a sound-deadening cubicle. Check squeaking floorboards and doors. 'Noise marshalls' should be delegated to control the back and sides of a room so that if, for example, waiters start chattering or clattering cutlery, they are immediately asked to stop.

Having studied the acoustics, decide where you are going to put your microphone, lectern, screen (if any) and stage. It is not good enough if people halfway down the room can't see. Try not to position your guests too far away from speakers or screens and position the seats and screen so that the entry doors are at the rear. This will prevent distraction from latecomers. A lectern should not be too far away from a screen otherwise the audience will have to swing backwards and forwards from screen to speaker. In addition a lecturer should be able to see the screen; it is dispiriting to give a talk and discover afterwards that the slides were all out of synchronisation. It is even more dispiriting when nobody notices.

Don't stand speakers in front of mirrors or wall lights (which may give them undeserved haloes) nor in front of windows; the outside light will distract your audience. Draw the curtains if no other position is suitable. Most hotels will be able to supply a lectern; some look like control units for space missions and are rarely essential, in fact they may be off-putting. Lecterns with built-in speakers are available but something simple, adjustable for height and angle with a light for notes (preferably with a dimmer control) should be adequate. Speakers must know where switches are. A lectern should be wide enough to take an A4-sized folder, open, with something such a simple strip of wood to stop it slipping off the bottom. Traffic lights on lecterns to signal speakers when to stop seem somewhat intimidating; the audience will tend to watch them rather than listen to the words. There should be a shelf on the lectern for a supply of water and a glass.

The eye level for presenters is important; if your speaker has to drop his eyes down too much to look at notes, he will lose eye contact with the audience. If speakers of different heights follow one another to the same lectern, and it is not adjustable, have a simple box for the shorter person to stand on. Where there are several presenters consider two lecterns on opposite sides of the room to speed up the flow and avoid speakers bumping into each other during changeovers. If there is only one, rehearse changeovers between speakers so that they get on and off without confusion. Remember to have some light for speakers as they move away from the spotlight, so that they don't fall over a step as a result of being plunged into darkness. However good the lighting on a lectern, play safe and have a torch (with a fresh battery) clipped to it.

Install the best public address you can find, and afford; a good system is essential to your audience's enjoyment. Move around the room while someone speaks from the stage to establish if you need a microphone; if in any doubt, get one. There will be more noise in a room with an audience present. Someone should be present who knows how to work the system; blowing into a microphone and shouting '1, 2, 3, testing' is not quite the image you should project. Apart from anything else, tapping and blowing into microphones may damage sensitive equipment (such as your sound man's ears). It is curious but, if a microphone gives problems, a speaker will often stop and gaze at it; unless they have extraordinary powers, looking at it is unlikely to cure it. Incidentally, the dreaded 'howl' or 'feedback' which gives audiences so much pleasure, and causes organisers so much anguish, is usually caused by the volume being turned up too high or by poor loudspeaker placement, so that the microphone picks up the loud speakers and starts a vicious circle. For speech, the sound should be set at the treble end which is the sharpest and therefore clearest.

A microphone should be mounted on a lectern and if a speaker is constantly turning his head towards a screen, two microphones may be needed, otherwise voices will keep fading. A halter mike hung round the neck may be best, although these take a little getting used to (at first speakers may feel that they are not working). Hand-held microphones are restrictive if a speaker needs to handle notes. Consider using radio microphones if your speaker needs to move around, say for a product presentation. There may be interference problems if you use more than three and you will need a licence to operate them in most areas.

At a dinner it is better to position microphones on banquet stands placed on tables in front of speakers. Tall floor-standing microphones may make them look like night club singers; it is easier to use notes if there is a table to rest them on.

The first announcement should be made with a microphone in order to attract the audience's attention and bring them to order.

Some conference venues have elaborate sound systems where each delegate has a microphone in front of him, fed through a central control box on the top table. These can be rather complicated and the chairman should know how to operate the system before a meeting starts.

When taking questions from an audience to put to speakers, you may need some way of amplifying them; long questions which cannot be heard at the back of the room can kill an occasion. Rifle microphones, which when pointed at questioners will pick up sound from 15 metres away, may be one solution; roving microphones may be passed along rows to questioners, but may take too long and slow the pace of an event. It is better to have an assistant at the back of a room who repeats questions to the chairman; he in turn should repeat questions anyway before inviting answers.

It is no use having splendid microphones if they are linked to a poor loudspeaker system. A speaker built in to a battered film projector will not be adequate for a large gathering. Get the best that is available in the area and use professional operators. They should know more about electrics than how to wire the lights on a Christmas tree, if police cars, taxis or even airport radar systems are not to come over on your public address system. An expert can work magic, distributing different levels of sound to people sitting further and further from the lectern, even building in a delay at the back to avoid echo.

Hiring or leasing equipment may be better than buying because it can get out of date very quickly. For the same reason, if an hotel assures you that it has the equipment you need – check it. Don't rely on pulling it out of a corner cupboard at the last minute. If you hire equipment, an operator must be present throughout the event in case of trouble; and stress to any hire firm that you want an operator who knows the equipment, not just a van driver who is a hi-fi enthusiast.

You can install stereo sound and if you are presenting a talk, say on railways, it may be impressive to move the sound of a train across the room; but for the average meeting stereo can become something of a producer's ego trip, as can quadrophonic sound.

By using cassette copiers you can give every delegate a tape of speeches soon after they have been delivered. I am not sure that the recipients ever play the tapes again, but it can be a nice touch. It is rude to record speakers without their permission; organisers tend to do this with after-dinner speakers, forgetting that, for a professional speaker, they may be stealing part of his livelihood.

Finally, does the room have enough electrical sockets and has your equipment adequate lengths of flex?

Panels

If you decide on a panel of speakers for a debate, or to answer questions, consider how to present them. Television chat shows love to have guests relaxing round a coffee table, but they are chat shows – you may have firmer messages to deliver, in which case a more formal setting at a table will be better. A chat show style could result in your production being too relaxed and low key. The table should be covered with felt and have ashtrays, water jugs, notepads and pencils and, above all, a modesty panel across the front; some guests have a distressing habit of scratching themselves in public.

If you are running a forum or panel session there should be one microphone per person. A long pause after a chairman has said 'What do you think, Joe?' during which Joe gets his neighbour's microphone and sorts out how to switch it on, will slow the pace and prevent the interchange between panel members which could make the function go with a swing. So, one microphone per speaker.

Speakers should be discouraged from banging on tables, as microphones will pick up the sound; for the same reason they should not beat their chests with pride.

If you have table microphones for a forum, have another one on a longer lead to be used for introducing the speakers. Bouncing onto the stage to do this, then having to bend double over the table to use one of the fixed microphones is not dignified.

A small point with panels: it is helpful if the chairman has a telephone link to a helper at the back of the hall who can be prompted to raise questions if the proceedings flag, or be asked to shut up a noisy barman etc.

Multi-lingual translations

Faced with the challenge of catering for delegates of different nationalities, remember the following points:

* Use professionals who should be briefed on the jargon and technicalities of your business. They should also be fully briefed on the format of your meeting so that, for instance, the changeover of interpreters fits in smoothly.
* Display the various language channels on a board at the front of the room, like a hymn list.
* Remember that all questions must go through the chairman (or, at the very least, everyone answering a question must repeat it), otherwise the interpreter won't be able to translate them.
* Consider using projection equipment with multi-tracks for different languages.

Music

Music can add a lot to an occasion; if you don't believe this, turn off the sound when next you watch a western on TV and see how little atmosphere there is. To set the mood for a function, play 'wallpaper music' (i.e. something fairly bland) as an audience moves into a room, as well as during coffee breaks and at any other times to kill a chilly silence; a simple tape recorder or record player plugged into your loudspeakers may be adequate in a small room. Almost anything is better than silence. If you create atmosphere with music and light, you will encourage speakers to 'switch on' and give better performances. Also you will need music during any reveal sequence, to add bite (or even to drown the noise of any machinery used during a sequence to reveal a new product to a breathless audience).

Music and the law

Copyright music performed in public by any means requires a licence. Without one you could be infringing someone's legal rights and liable to pay damages.

Generally in the UK where sound recordings are played for public performances, two licences may be required. Public performance refers to anything other than home use, so although a private club might pick its membership, any performance of records on its premises would be a public performance.

Phonographic Performance Limited looks after the public performance and broadcasting of commercial sound recordings on behalf of the British record industry. The Performing Rights Society, on the other hand, looks after the public performance and broadcasting of the composer's music, so although their licence is more often required when live music is played, they are also involved with record use since records contain some composers' copyright music.

The above applies to all forms of sound recordings obtained through normal shops, but if at any time you propose to re-record onto blank tapes for any purpose, you will need permission from The Mechanical Copyright

Protection Society Limited. These organisations are all British; corresponding ones exist in other parts of the world.

There may be similar complications in clearing video recordings, particularly if music is involved, although you may be less likely to be using such footage in a conference.

Complicated? Perhaps, but outside consultants will handle the details without any problem, as will most venue owners. Charges are not high and registered charities and similar bodies may qualify for exemption under the provisions of the Copyright Act.

Recognisable music, e.g. something that has been in the Top Ten, can add colour or impact to a function, but is more difficult to clear copyright and more expensive to use than 'library music' which is specially composed incidental music pre-recorded on disc. You can get a musical acompaniment for almost any kind of scene and it is not expensive.

Lighting

Know where the light switches are and delegate someone to stay near them throughout your function. It helps to create atmosphere if lights are on dimmer switches so make full use of this facility if available; dimming house lights so that all eyes are on a speaker who is spotlit; lowering lights for dancing etc. However, lights yo-yoing up and down all the time will give your audience eye strain.

You may want to do a *son et lumière* on your board of directors or VIPs on a top table; try to create enough atmosphere to distinguish them without having so many spotlights on them that they fry. In order to spotlight particular people in the audience, for example when introducing celebrities, seat them in pre-arranged places or at the very least have someone sitting alongside the lighting man who knows who's who; it looks amateurish to have spotlights swerving about trying to locate a guest.

Spotlights sometimes require support towers, otherwise they will be directed into speakers' eyes. If it is a questions session, speakers may not be able to see an audience if lights are too bright; you may have to bring the house lights up a little.

Don't light speakers directly from behind, otherwise the audience won't be able to see them, nor from above, because they will look like Frankenstein's monster.

Discourage speakers from wearing plastic badges or flashy jewellery which may reflect light and distract the audience.

Colour filters in your lighting plans can add atmosphere, and remember that audiences are conditioned to expect signals from the lighting. For example, lights going down means something is going to happen – don't disappoint them.

When you have placed the sound and lighting, see if you can make it all look neater, perhaps by fixing cables in place with sticky tape. Too often there are unsightly wires trailing all over the place.

Finally, remember that electricity can be dangerous. Obvious, of course, but too often you read of people, particularly pop musicians, being electrocuted, so take care.

16 Visual aids

Research suggests that we retain 10 per cent of what we read, 20 per cent of what we hear and 50 per cent of what we see and hear together, which indicates that the effective use of visual aids can help retention.

The most important visual aid at a function is a well presented room which will relax delegates and put them in a receptive frame of mind. Dress a room, if necessary, with point-of-sale material, banners, flowers or screens, blocking off dead or discouraging areas where possible. Put up display material in any coffee areas and use your conference logo or company symbol as part of the display.

If delegates are to concentrate on a screen showing films or slides, do what you can to keep out light. If there is a stage, make sure that it is solid and will take your display material. Blackboards, screens or lecterns must be clearly visible – check the sightlines from all parts of the room after the stage has been built. Get the best technical equipment you can afford, with skilled operators who will know what lenses to use etc. Equipment should be firmly mounted on proper stands; projectors should not rest on beer crates.

Presenting information

When presenting information, aim for clarity. If an audience is puzzled by a visual aid, such as a chart, your message won't register. Don't display irrelevant information or anything which is not being referred to by the speaker. Information should be given in the manner in which it is easiest to absorb; for example columns of figures should be in ascending order. And be consistent; if you show years horizontally on one chart, don't put them vertically on the next. You may use bar charts, 3D bars, graphs, pie charts or some you've invented, but consistency of style is desirable. Don't patronise your audience – twee loaves and little fishes to represent your annual accounts may be just too much.

Use colour, say one to represent Government action, a second to show company activity, perhaps with a third to show other forces impacting on your affairs.

Don't fudge or lie when making illustrations. Facts must be honest or you will destroy your credibility, so don't fake graphs so that sales figures look more dramatic than they really are.

Figures on a screen must be the same as in a script; if 6315 shows on the screen but the speaker refers to 6314 or 6316, the slight difference will tend to puzzle the audience.

Screens

Tailor the screen to the audience, not to your projector; as a rough guide, twice the screen width should equal the distance from the screen to the people sitting in the front row while, ideally, the last row of the audience should not be more than six times the screen width away from the screen. A projectionist will be interested in how far away the projector is from the screen, how big a picture the screen will take and, finally, the lens focal length (which can be varied by changing the lens or using a zoom). If he knows two of these three facts he can find the third from a simple chart and set up his equipment accordingly.

There are screens which have been specially designed for daylight viewing while, if space is short, a translucent screen allowing projection from the back is useful because it keeps the projector out of the room containing the audience. Depending on the angle of the projector, it may be necessary to lean the top of the screen forwards slightly to remove any distortion of the image shown.

Prompting aids

Increasingly, speakers are turning to prompting aids to smooth their performance. There are several systems which are, in effect, closed circuit televisions. A speech is typed onto a long roll of paper which is then placed under a camera lens in a control unit positioned off-stage. An operator feeds the unit at the speaker's pace and the words appear on a piece of plain glass on the lectern in front of the speaker's eyes. All he or she has to do is read aloud. It really is as simple as that; if you can read you can do it. (It is arguable that with some speakers the glass should be armour plated.)

If a speaker needs simple prompting aids, say for a television interview, there is nothing wrong with 'idiot cards' – large boards, with key points scribbled on them, held near to the camera. Comedians even write notes on shirt cuffs but this may be messy for a conference speaker.

Blackboards

Children have been taught with blackboards for generations and they may still have a place in conferences. Yellow chalk is better than white and, as with other visual aids, use different colours to indicate different things. A damp cloth should be used to clean blackboards to avoid a shower of chalk and horrible squeaks.

A complicated chart should be drawn in advance of the conference, then rubbed out leaving a faint trace; the lecturer can then draw it again with confidence in front of the audience by following the marks.

Other boards

Other types of board include white rather than black-boards; pinboards (perhaps pinning up point-of-sale material); boards which take felt tip pens or stick on symbols; and boards with lines, squares etc. already printed on them. Or magnetic boards can be used; and there are double-sided boards which are magnetic on one side and blackboards on the other – the permutations are endless. All these tend to be less intimate than a good old-fashioned blackboard but they are slightly more elegant.

Flip-over charts

For fairly small groups, simple flip-over charts with illustrations drawn on cards or paper, mounted on a table or easel, can be perfectly acceptable. Cover the first chart with a plain sheet or company logo until the presentation starts. As with blackboards, if drawings have to be made, pencil them in lightly beforehand so that they can be drawn quickly and neatly later in front of an audience.

When using plain paper for flip-over charts, have a box or bin for scrap paper otherwise the venue will quickly become cluttered.

Overhead projectors

Overhead projectors always seem a shade schoolmasterish and are perhaps better for lectures than general presenta-tions. They are cruder than slides and unsuitable for really large audiences but are low cost, may be portable, and no blackout is needed (although you should not put the screen in bright sunlight). A presenter can face his audience, maintain eye contact and readily gauge reaction to his words.

Transparencies are made by writing on transparent acetate sheets with special felt tip pens or chinagraph pencils. Use stencils for lettering if your handwriting is poor, although the casual air of handwritten material is perhaps part of the charm of an overhead projector.

Information can be photocopied on to transparency film using special copiers (strides are being made in this area so, if you are interested in buying something, do check the latest state of the art). Transparencies can be up to A4 size and card masks can be put over part of an illustration so that a speaker can gradually reveal, say, a chart as his lecture proceeds.

Charts can be improved by using coloured adhesive film and it is even possible to devise simple schemes to animate illustrations.

Slides

Slides are next up the pecking order of visual aids. They are far and away the most popular method of presenting information and therefore Chapter 17 is devoted to them.

Film strips

Film strips are a sequence (usually 20–40 pictures) of transparencies on 35mm film and are widely used for teaching, training and selling. Commercial film strips in both colour and black and white are available together with ready produced notes for lectures on various subjects. The big advantage of film strip, unlike slides, is that the pictures can't get out of sequence.

Films

Perhaps the greatest advantage of films is that they are

easily transported and relatively cheap, while projectors are standard around the world; all of which makes films ideal for international business communication. The disadvantage is that they are slower to produce than videos.

To add a professional touch to a business function, you can hire excellent training films but link them properly into the rest of the meeting; don't run them in isolation. When hiring films, remember that black and white looks very old fashioned nowadays although it is perfectly acceptable for historical films.

If you have a special film made which someone 'talks to' during a presentation, rehearse it well because such ideas are acutely embarrassing if they go wrong. It is possible to talk over silent films to add a commentary but, again, this must be carefully rehearsed.

If using only part of a film, get it positioned so that it is ready to start at the point you want. Be sure the operator knows exactly what is required.

If you are using extracts from different films, splice them together with a coloured leader of about 15 seconds between each one, which will give a lecturer time to link the sections; this method is much better than constantly switching projectors on and off. The projectionist may need to adjust his focusing for the different sections.

A film is of little use without a projector of course. Normally you will be using 16mm film, although it is possible to get adequate quality from super 8. If you move the other way, to 35mm, there may be problems in some places where authorities insist on fireproof projection booths and other safeguards (a throwback to the days when film was made of cellulose nitrate and was highly flammable).

Modern projectors are almost idiot proof, but although they will lace themselves and do other clever things you should still have a skilled operator with you.

Loop films can be used for training or continuous display, say in a coffee area. As the name suggests, a loop film has its ends joined so that it can be run continuously.

Video

Video is now taken for granted and, I suspect, will take over from film completely as bigger screens become freely and cheaply available. You can now get up to 40-foot screens for television although they are expensive; nevertheless LSV (large screen video) just has to become more popular. As an alternative to a large screen at the end of a room, it is possible to have a battery of linked television sets showing the same material, although this method tends to pull people's eyes from the main speaker.

Video is quicker to produce than film and is easier to show in daylight, but remember that people are used to professional standards from watching television at home – they may expect similar standards at your function. Technically your video may not need to be of broadcast quality but amateur video may aesthetically be worse than none at all.

Graphics can now be made quickly by computer and various other tricks can be used to add brightness to a video presentation. If you add a computer captioner to a linked TV system, you can put up the morning sales figures or other information during a conference. You can also add arrows, circles or whatever to a video presentation. But take care; there are quite a few cowboys in this area. You don't need any qualifications to set up as a video producer so select one with your eyes firmly open.

A fairly major problem with video is that the industry is still scrapping over compatibility. It is possible to transfer material from one cassette system to another, but this is an added complication. Film can also be transferred to video, and vice versa, although video to film may not give very good quality.

Video discs

With this system, a laser beam scans a disc rather like a silver LP record. One disc holds 54,000 'pages' of information; any page can be reached in a couple of seconds and a disc can be programmed to go backwards and forwards over a particular sequence, say for training or display. Slow/fast motion and freeze frame can be used and sound reproduction is excellent. But there are snags. Material has to be pre-recorded (you can't record onto your own discs) and there are compatibility problems between systems.

Other visual aids

Large blow up photographs can make useful visual aids if used to illustrate, say, part of a machine or a new factory layout.

Models may have their place in a function: model girls to hand round cigarettes, show clothes or hold up a particularly boring product; and scale models of factories or products.

Entertainment. Ready-made humorous films are available to introduce coffee breaks and other aspects of a function and can add light relief, as can *cartoon characters* specially designed for projection on a video screen. Characters can be created for specific purposes and can be programmed to operate 'live' with the character talking to the audience. They can be particularly effective at exhibitions hailing passers-by.

Lasers were something of a non-event when they were first introduced but they now have their uses in major and dramatic presentations. Remember that lasers are silent so they need music for maximum effect. Above all, don't fool with them, don't prod them with screwdrivers if they go wrong, don't look along them to see why they aren't working. Obey all the local regulations regarding their use. They are not something for amateurs.

Holograms are in effect completely three-dimensional photographs. The result is that you feel you can actually reach out and hold something, which you then find isn't there. Holograms are quite dramatic but may eventually be taken for granted; they are more useful in display areas than at a conference itself.

Talking heads involve projecting a specially prepared film onto a sculpture of someone's head with the result that it appears that the person is actually present. They are dramatic, particularly if a celebrity's head is used, although as more and more appear their effect will become less sensational.

Radio-controlled robots, perhaps in the shape of a product pack, can be moved among an audience (say, during a coffee break) or featured in a presentation. They can be programmed to speak different languages.

Here are a few final points on visual aids:

* If you are planning for someone to burst through a paper screen (showing a film or slide) to launch a new product, do rehearse the timing and get it right – or don't do it.
* If you have a new company TV commercial, show it during a meeting, perhaps as an attention grabber after a break. Remember that commercials will be more dramatic if shown on a big screen.
* If you are giving presentations around the world, always do a local rehearsal; equipment may be standard but mains electricity supplies may not. Tape and video machines will run at the wrong speed if they have been designed for the UK 50 Htz supply and are used on a 60 Htz supply in America or Japan.
* Before you start a presentation abroad, check there are no local union problems. In some countries slide men may not operate cine, in others someone may have to read the script to cue the slide operator. You won't be able to change local industrial relations practices overnight, but you may at least be able to stop the plug being pulled out at a key point.
* Be very cautious about introducing slides,

video or films during an after-dinner speech;
they will usually be inappropriate.

There does seem an awful lot to say on the technicalities of visual aids. So much remarkable equipment is available that, eventually, a 'come as you are' conference with a good speaker at the blackboard will be hailed as a communications breakthrough. You will be able to serve natural foods and Real Ale too.

If you find the march of technology too much for you, don't despair. A good speaker perched on the end of a table with a hand microphone can still be the most effective communicator if he is sincere and has a clear idea of what he wants to say. Provided the table doesn't collapse of course. . . .

17 Slides

Slides are far and away the most popular (and most abused) visual aid but before considering the ubiquitous 35mm slide, think for a moment of the projector; as with any technical equipment, use good quality products with experienced operators.

Some people become neurotic about bulb failure in a projector but if a bulb is working leave it alone; a new one is just as likely to fail (have a spare bulb or two at hand, of course). Bulbs tend to fail when first switched on because their resistance is lowest when they are cold, but if a blank slide is inserted earlier, so that the projector can be switched on before a presentation starts, the projectionist will be certain that the bulb is working.

There should be one or two slides at the front of a slide tray to use to focus the projector, rather similar to test cards used on television. Use spare slides from the actual presentation or, preferably, test slides with special graphics (you will definitely need these if you are using more than one projector). A good projectionist may use a telescope to focus slides properly if he is operating a long way from the screen.

Remember that a projectionist will need light to read a script if he is operating the slide changes.

If you are using slides and have wallpaper music playing as an audience filters into an auditorium, put up a series of attractive slides, either of a product or something relevant to the company (or just pretty pictures) to relax people and set the mood. The sequence should end with a company or conference logo as the start time approaches.

Money is often wasted on slides through lack of planning. Sort out the running order of a presentation then do rough sketches of possible slides. Talk through the presentation with the sketches on display to establish that the proposed illustrations work then, and only then, commission art work for slides. Remember the order: words then slides.

Executives will not need to be reminded to get sensitive information cleared around the company before they make expensive slides. With confidential information you may need to consider the security arrangements of any slide making company you use.

Slides are colourful, but a relentless flow may send an audience to sleep. Vary the pace of your meeting if you can, possibly by having someone speak without slides (with the house lights up) between two elaborate slide presentations.

The quality of slides is more important than the quantity so give a lot of thought to their preparation, bearing the following in mind:

* A slide that can't be read is worse than none at all.
* Have a house style for your slides and use the same typeface for all of them.
* Sans serif type should be used; if slides are being made from typewritten material, it should be double spaced.
* Don't keep swapping between horizontal and vertical slides because it is distracting; preferably slides should be landscape shaped, i.e. wider than they are deep.

* A slide tray holds 80 slides, so don't have a presentation using 81 or 161.
* There should never be more than 15 to 20 words or 25 to 30 numbers on a slide; use more than one slide if necessary, rather than make one unduly complicated.
* Don't put key figures at the bottom of a slide because, despite all warnings about screen heights, people at the back won't be able to see. If you are likely to be transferring a slide show to video later, don't put information too near the edges of the slides; it won't show on TV screens.
* Dark backgrounds show up information better, and flaw less, than light ones.
* White letters on a blue background or black letters on a yellow background are effective as are other strongly contrasting combinations. Avoid soft toning colours, the slides may be indistinct.
* Engineering and architectural drawings tend to make poor slides.
* If you have to use old photographs for an illustration, consider giving them a colour tint to make them look less ancient.
* Computer-produced graphics for slides are quick to make and very acceptable to generations brought up on Space Invaders.

Slides should be mounted in plastic rather than card because heat can cause card to buckle and throw a slide out of focus. Clean slides before use, or they may look like police fingerprint records; even minor faults will show up when magnified umpteen times. Hold slides by the edges, or handle them with soft gloves, and use a light-box to sort them into order. Draw up a 'slide sheet', a list of the slides in order, preferably with rough sketches as a reminder of the slide illustrations. If a slide is missing during rehearsal, put a blank in its place with a scribbled comment in felt tip to say what it represents; put the correct one in place before the presentation.

Build-up slides showing first one piece of information then two etc., may help to put over complicated information but they need close co-ordination between the speaker and operator. Such slides must not jump as you move from one to the next; use a register when the slides are made and place them in special registration mounts. However, although a series of build-up slides may help to impart information, don't get too carried away; it looks absurd to put up one slide saying 'good' then another saying 'morning' then a third saying 'good morning gentlemen'. It has been known.

When rehearsing a slide presentation, don't cling to a favourite slide if it is clearly irrelevant. If at a certain place in the presentation no slide is available, switch to a company or conference logo (or a colour tint) rather than a blank screen or, worse, an irrelevant slide. If you need to show a slide twice, duplicate it. Never try to go back to find it again. For an important presentation, it is worth having a complete set of spare slides in case of emergency.

When slides have been sorted into sequence, number them clearly then double check that they are in the correct order. If you are using a pair of projectors, one slide tray will take slides 1, 3, 5, 7 etc. while the second takes 2, 4, 6, 8. For several slide trays, use additional identification, e.g. A, B, C etc.

Scripts

The script for a slide presentation should be kept in a ringed binder so that it is easy to turn over the pages. The projectionist should have a copy of the script, perhaps with a special page at the front spelling out how the cues operate and warning of any likely snags. If a presenter chooses to cue the operator each time he wants a slide changed, a signalling button is preferable to saying 'can we have the next slide please'. Chat between presenter and operator tends to destroy any magic. A presenter may prefer to operate the projector himself by remote control. Slides can be moved forwards and backwards and focused by remote control although, for the latter, the presenter must have a clear view of the screen. Slide change points should be marked boldly in a script, or a presenter may forget them if he gets too carried away by his own eloquence.

Marking a script for slide presentation is really a matter of personal preference. You can underline the words in the script (perhaps with a coloured felt tip pen) on which you want a slide change, or put a stroke through the script, or circle key words. A good projectionist may ask you simply to mark exactly where you want the fresh slide to appear on the screen, leaving him to decide when to press the button, according to the equipment he is using and individual reading speeds. When using one projector it takes about 1.7 seconds for a slide to change; with a dissolve system with two or more projectors the change can be immediate.

It helps if a presenter knows what is, or should be, on the screen at any given time so put sketches of the slides at appropriate points in the script. One page of script per slide may be used, but this involves much page turning. Use whichever system suits you, but be consistent otherwise you will confuse the projectionist or, worse, the audience if your timing goes wrong. Scripts should be at least double spaced and neatly typed (think of the projectionist who may be in semi-darkness) and at all times the words must relate to the slides.

If you are a pessimist, with little faith in projectors, you will go through a script before delivering it and consider how to cope if a bulb fails or there is a power cut. Remember the following points with slide presentations:

* Presenters should be cautious of ad libbing unless the projectionist has been warned or they are operating the slide changes themselves.
* Care with the use of cartoons as slide illustrations – they can work, but too often they don't. Known cartoonists with recognisable styles may be the most acceptable.
* A picture of the speaker (with his name and

title) could be shown on the screen as he
starts to speak; an audience should always
know who is addressing them. The slide
should be removed after a few seconds.

* World-weary professionals may complain
  that presentations to male audiences, such as
  salesmen, always include girly pictures. Don't
  knock it, it may be the only slide show a salesforce sees all year.

* When numbering slides, avoid adding 9A, 9B
  etc. because this may confuse a projectionist,
  particularly if you wish to refer back to a slide
  during a discussion after presentation.

* When planning your presentation, vary the
  length of time for showing each slide. Sound
  and pictures should be balanced, so don't
  drone on for too long over one slide.

Slide-tape

With slide-tape presentations, simple pulses on the sound
tape operate the projector. Watch the compatibility of the
pulsing and equipment you are using and have an operator
standing by during a slide-tape show ready to operate the
manual override if things get out of phase.

With modern techniques, using multi-projectors, slide
sequences can be animated to provide movements similar
to film. (So why not use film? Because slides can give a
totally different effect.) However don't go wild on slide
technology; it may result in blurring your basic messages.

Twin projectors cut out the blank gaps between slides
and are more sophisticated than just one projector; but
they can be more trouble too if someone drops a slide tray,
and are not really essential for a small audience. You can
add a third projector to circle a figure on a chart but again,
this is not essential. If three aren't essential, neither are 20
or 50 projectors. Elaborate slide presentations can be
exhilarating, but if you use them, don't let the technology
swamp your message. Use professionals to operate the

equipment, but don't be frightened by their jargon. Get them to explain exactly what they are doing and then you will detect if they have considered their ideas thoroughly. The effects of wide screens, split screens, dissolves, fades, computer controlled slides etc. can be thrilling but they can also run away with costs and destroy any advantage in flexibility which slides should have over film or video. If you have to freeze a slide presentation too early because everything has to be locked into a computer then perhaps it is time to consider a simpler system.

Incidentally, even multi-projectors that are computer programmed still depend on gravity for their final slide operation. Newton would have liked that.

18 Printing

The quality of the printed material received by delegates says something about your organisation, so get the best you can afford. Competition in the printing world is fierce and you should obtain more than one quotation. Remember that printers may have their own suggestions for improvements.

Don't waste money on printing. The cost of an invitation card will go up by 50 per cent if you have embossed lettering, and by 90 per cent if you have two colours; ask yourself if this is really necessary. The cheapest way of adding variety may be to vary the colour of the paper.

Consider a special logo for an important conference which should be properly designed, not doodled on the back of an envelope by the managing director.

Notepaper

Special notepaper or a label promoting the event to stick on existing paper may be appropriate for a large function.

Where several organisers are using special conference paper, have a 'please reply to' line at the top with space for their own addresses. You may consider special envelopes, with the same logo on them, although I sometimes feel that these only appeal to postmen and mail clerks.

Letters must be well typed. A word processor will be invaluable if you have to write similar letters to all of your many delegates, with perhaps minor changes over travel arrangements. The tone of your letter will set the style for your event. An invitation letter which is full of brusque timing details and little else will hardly encourage people to attend.

Invitations

Your invitations must spell out what, where and when. For social functions you should state whether it is evening dress or optional; ladies in particular will want this information and if dress is optional at least give more guidance to any guests on the top table.

A finishing time on invitations will help guests to plan transport and either the invitation or ticket should give directions for finding a venue if it is difficult for strangers to an area. It is courteous to point out one-way systems and parking areas and to state the distance of the venue from the station. All this sort of information can be put onto a separate sheet to avoid cluttering invitation cards. There should be an RSVP on tickets and an address for replies; ready-printed reply paid postcards will help to ensure rapid return.

Unusual invitations may increase your acceptance rate, e.g. a cut-out plate for a dinner invitation could be expensive but quite an attention grabber.

Conference material

Any brochures, leaflets or letters concerning a conference

must reflect the style of the event and be well prepared, as should any final instructions sent to delegates. The latter should include the telephone number of the venue in case of emergency and for overseas functions special conference luggage labels should be included for quick identification.

Any material handed out at the conference itself should be in a spiral bound book or folder, possibly with the logo embossed on it. Such holders should always be designed so that they are suitable for delegates' children afterwards, as they will rarely be used otherwise and, for that reason, gold blocking of individual names on them may be unnecessarily gilding the plastic.

Different coloured paper may be used for instructions for different days of a long conference; but avoid duplication or a plethora of printer papers – you will just overload delegates. However, if they are staying overnight there should be a letter of welcome in every room, recapping on the main points of the programme. Prepare this letter as late as possible in case of last-minute changes in the programme, although you must allow time for duplicating, collating and distribution. It is helpful to hand out a plan of the venue along with room keys if it is vast and confusing; a list of delegates will also be appreciated. A literature rack may be necessary if there are company or association publications to be distributed or sold.

Copies of speeches given out in advance may lower the attention level of delegates. One alternative is to distribute sheets containing just the main section headings with space underneath for delegates' own notes; another solution is to put out notepads and leave delegates to make their own record. The chairman should always explain what, if any, method is to be used. Although some organisations send out a record of conferences to delegates afterwards, I am not convinced that people ever read transcripts of speeches etc. although back-up material on complicated subjects may be useful.

Badges

It is helpful if guests can readily identify each other at a function and badges should be issued if necessary although not, of course, for formal dinners. There are many different types of badge to choose from. Most common perhaps are badges which slip into the breast pockets of jackets but they are of no use if it is hot and people take their jackets off; those with clips or safety pins are more versatile. Some are designed to display visiting cards although you really need a bigger type face so that names can be read easily. More up-market badges may have the company name or logo engraved on them along with delegates' names (or you can use Dymotape to add names). Perhaps best of all are stick-on fabric badges (with names typed on) which can be stuck onto jackets, ties or shirts and, for that matter, onto blouses or dresses. Delegates may need more than one of these badges for a long conference because they can get frayed at the edges.

Use a large typewriter face or print badges, but don't hand-write them, unless you can do copperplate they will look scruffy. Different coloured badges may be convenient for each section of the organising team for reasons of identification or security (if the latter, be sure security staff know the code).

If possible, carry the theme of your function onto the badges; if you are holding a wild west affair name badges could be in the shape of cowboy hats or sheriffs' stars.

Officials may wear flowers in their buttonholes as identification; this method is particularly appropriate at a formal dinner.

Tickets

Guests are rarely asked for tickets at functions, but if you insist on them let the printing reflect the style of your event. They should be a convenient size to go in handbags or the pocket of a suit. Tickets may be numbered for control purposes or if you are planning to hold a raffle based on the numbers.

In order to control admissions, you must have someone with tact on the door because a percentage of guests will have forgotten their tickets.

Table plans

A table plan is desirable for any dinner involving more than a handful of people, otherwise the meal will get off to a bad start as guests mill about. For a large attendance, there should be more than one table plan. Mount them high up in the cocktail area where they can be easily seen, with large letters so that guests don't need their reading glasses to discover where they are sitting. The smoothest system is for every guest to be handed a table plan, preferably on fairly flimsy paper which can be tucked into a pocket. If possible use people's first names and add the names of delegates' companies; as well as listing guests in alphabetical order with their table numbers, consider listing table groupings so that they can tell at a glance who they are sitting with.

It helps 'traffic flow' if a table plan shows a floor plan of the tables, preferably including any stage or doors to help guests orientate themselves.

Place cards

If you plan the seating for a dinner then you must have cards at each place setting; for a more relaxed affair it may be acceptable to have them for top table only, leaving other guests to sit where they wish. Place cards must be typed or printed and ideally they should feature the company or event logo; they should either be folded over so that they are free-standing or be laid flat on top of a wine glass. To save printing costs, a space for names to be added can be incorporated onto the front of menus. An added refinement for place cards at a business function is to have lines saying 'on your left is. . .' (then a gap for a name and company to be filled in) and 'on your right is. . .'. However, avoid this if there are likely to be last-minute changes.

Menus

Menus should be well presented because they are on display more than most printed material.

List the wines (if you are proud of them) as well as any toasts, so that guests know what agonies are in store for them. Use first names for those who are proposing toasts or making speeches. It is courteous to include the name of a toastmaster and there is no reason why you should not add details of tombolas, raffles, etc., on the menu.

If you want to lighten an evening, put a cartoon or picture on the back of the menu with space for people to write their own captions with prizes for the best (remember that as the wine takes hold, entries will become ribald).

Menus can be printed on the sides of toy cars or beer tankards or other items which make souvenir gifts.

Miscellaneous printed material

Other printed material may be needed as follows:

* Direction and 'reserved' signs; these should be printed rather than scribbled on pieces of card.
* 'No smoking' signs.
* Book matches, with a company or conference logo.
* Table numbers (although the venue will usually be able to supply these).
* Name cards, in large type, to identify members of a speaking panel; have a flip-over system if you wish to keep an audience in suspense until star panellists appear.
* Meaningless certificates certifying that delegates have done such-and-such (even

performed with valour against overwhelming sales odds) tend to get framed and displayed if they are sufficiently tongue-in-cheek.
* Souvenir pictures. If you have a rapid processing system hand them out as guests leave, otherwise mail them later.

Press releases

Special press release paper is desirable if you want to make an impact; at the very least, overprint or put stickers on existing A4 notepaper. Type press releases; don't print them as this makes the news look old. Press releases need double spacing and should be typed on one side of the paper, with generous margins. Keep them simple with sentences and paragraphs short; include all the facts, use straightforward language and avoid jargon. Get names right! Give the day, date and time of your event and where it is. State if there is any charity involvement; the press may be more lavish in their coverage. Look for any unusual angle, preferably a local one, such as that a particular speaker is going to attack a controversial local project.

At the end of any release, type 'end' so that journalists do not search for other pages. Include the name and telephone number of a contact for further information.

When you are promoting a conference or function via press releases, don't fire all your bullets at once. First send out a press release with a preliminary announcement of the event then later, nearer the date, announce that so-and-so has agreed to speak or that a certain celebrity will be attending. If possible, photographs of speakers should be sent out in advance. In fact, mail photographs of anything which may help to get press coverage – even an unusual trophy to be awarded to a star salesman. Photographs should be recent, at least 8" × 6" and black and white. There is no harm in including your firm's name in photographs, but not too ostentatiously otherwise they won't be used. Photographs should be clearly captioned (with identification from left to right) and captions should fill out and elaborate the pictures. Mail photographs in stout envelopes and mark then 'copyright free' so that newspapers know where they stand.

In the total cost of a function, postage stamps, envelopes and paper will be relatively minor items, so press releases should be mailed as widely as possible; send them to local radio stations, county magazines, trade magazines and, of course, to newspapers over a wide area.

19 On the day

The mark of a good organiser is that everything happens on cue and guests are unaware of all the effort going on behind the scenes. This chapter is something of a reprise of points made earlier in the book and in fact some of the points are repeated again in the Checklists to follow. This is an indication of the importance of planning and attention to detail if a function is to succeed.

Before guests arrive

General

When all your plans are made don't relax; Sod's Law will guarantee that something will go wrong. If you are on the alert, you are more likely to be able to cope. Needless to say, you should have contingency plans for the most likely upsets, such as a speaker failing to turn up or rain when you have planned a cocktail party on the lawn.

For any event, a banner hung outside or a message on a

venue noticeboard welcoming guests is a pleasant touch. There should be a doorman with an umbrella in the parking area if it is raining and car park attendants should be briefed not to be officious.

All support staff must be in position well ahead of your official start time – always assume that some guests will be at least half an hour early – and they should be given a worksheet which spells out exactly what happens when. For an important conference this 'worksheet' could develop into quite a large book. Workers should be briefed to stay in position and not disappear to chat with friends amongst the delegates; obviously you should plan to relieve staff for meal breaks, etc. If you are using a large venue, radio links between key officials are essential.

Remember the following points before guests arrive:

* Cleaners should tidy rooms, removing old cups and other debris left after any last rehearsals.

* Room heating should be adjusted properly, bearing in mind that bodies will raise the temperature.

* Cloakrooms should be open; tipping arrangements should be sorted out; toilets should be clean and basins should have spare towels.

* A final check should be made that no public address system, telephones or other noises can disrupt your function. I have laboured this point but extraneous noises are the bane of an organiser's life – if a hotel manager's child is teething and starts crying, if his labrador is lonely and starts howling, if his budgerigar gets broody and starts banging its bell, you have my word that it will happen at a crucial point for you. Be on your guard.

* If admission to the function is via pay-at-the-door, there should be a cash float with some arrangement made for security.

At dinners

* The tableplan should be up-to-date and clearly displayed.
* Place cards, menus and flowers should be in position on tables.
* Any wine-ordering system should be ready to operate; wine should be ordered for top table guests.
* Musicians and cabaret artists should be briefed.
* The organiser should discuss with the toast-master exactly what he is to say. Never leave this to the toastmaster's discretion or you may get unpleasant surprises, such as an attempt by him to start a round of applause at an inappropriate moment. Toastmasters tend to be 'characters' (I suppose they have to be to do their job), but you are paying so don't let them dominate you.

At meetings and conferences

* Rehearsals of speeches, product introductions etc. should, ideally, be some days before the date of your function (while there is still time to make major changes) but if, for some reason, you have to live dangerously and rehearse 'on the day' then do it very early and, if you are in this unhappy situation, don't plan an elaborate package that really needs more time.
* As well as cleaners sweeping rooms for litter before an audience files in, consider 'sweeping' the room for bugs in view of the growth of industrial espionage.
* There should be plenty of ashtrays and, ideally, signs should be in place indicating non-smoking areas.
* Slides should be cleaned and all technical

equipment given a final check.
* Water should be placed on tables or lecterns.
* There should be a message board for delegates.
* Have a basket of coins so that people can get change for telephones.
* Assuming that some delegates will be early, consider a flask of coffee in advance of the hotel's main supply; have newspapers available.
* Reserved seats should be marked.

When guests arrive

General

Delegate someone to watch for, and look after, key guests; if possible, keep VIPs away from the general audience, particularly if their presence is intended to be a surprise (even if not, speakers may prefer to relax rather than get involved with guests wanting to chat).

Senior personnel present should go out of their way to make newcomers feel welcome. All guests should be guided to the right room by someone pointing the way and adding 'we hope you enjoy the event'. As guests arrive, delegate someone to do a head count. If you find you are light on numbers for a dinner, consider removing one table, if seating is informal, because it will spoil the effect in a room if every table has empty places; for a conference, block off seats at the back or sides if you are down on numbers.

At dinners

* If a toastmaster announces guests, this should be after they have deposited coats in the cloakrooms.
* Guests are usually called for dinner 15–20 minutes after the start time shown on tickets, but liaise with the caterers and toastmaster

over this. If for any reason you plan to start exactly on time, guests should be warned of this on the tickets because it isn't common practice.

* If you call the main body of guests in before the top table, remember not to keep them waiting too long while VIPs finish their drinks in a private room.

At meetings and conferences

* Have an efficient registration system ready with your fieldforce on hand, if necessary, to identify strangers.
* Identification badges should be laid out in alphabetical order; if badges are being typed as guests register there should be plenty of typists.
* If it is a large event, keep delegates out of the main conference room until you are ready for them. And check that things are ready before delegates are shepherded in; don't have guests watching any last minute panics.
* Delegates should be shown into an auditorium with torches if there are dangerously dark areas.
* Unlike a dinner, aim to start a meeting or conference exactly on time to set an efficient tone for the proceedings.

During the event

General

* Always keep venue staff well informed of any change in your timing; if the chief guest is late or if a coffee break is going to be early, then let staff know.
* 'Noise marshals' should be present to prevent distractions during the programme. They

must be ready to stop any noise, much of which may come from your own, or the hotel's, staff whispering at the back. Somehow a whisper is more distracting than a louder noise.

* Brief company people to act as 'applause leaders' at appropriate moments.
* As the event progresses, change the programme if appropriate. For example, if a dance is clearly an outstanding success and you have booked an unknown comedian for a cabaret spot and are not too sure of his abilities, have the courage to cancel the act, provided it has not been billed on the menu.
* Don't read out obscure telegrams or messages with 'in' jokes if they are likely to puzzle the majority of guests.
* A chairman should never give the main speaker's speech; he should not say 'we have invited Mr Jones to tell us about A, B, and C' and then proceed to tell everyone about A, B, and C, himself.
* If there is an important incident just before or during your event, you may need to acknowledge it with an announcement and if, say, it is the death of the founder of the company, with a minute's silence.
* During the event, carry out some quick market research for future guidance by asking delegates for their views on the function.
* As the event progresses, check with railway stations or airports that speakers' return travel plans are still possible.

At dinners

* Let people know what is going on with announcements, e.g. 'That ends the formal part of the evening'.

* Have a break if people are faced with long speeches because they won't concentrate too well if they have to keep crossing their legs. If you have a 'comfort break', announce that 'Speeches will start in ten minutes', rather than 'There will now be a ten-minute break'. The latter will cause more people to get up, the toilets will be crowded and your proceedings will be delayed longer.
* Check that speakers are ready to rise before introducing them and also that serving staff are out of the room.
* Don't let a prizegiving drag on so long that it kills the flow of your dinner.
* A band should be ready to play (or disco ready to start) as soon as the formal part of an evening is over.
* Ask one or two company personnel to start the dancing or you may have an empty floor for most of the evening. Lights should be dimmed when dancing starts to make the atmosphere more intimate.
* Plan what, if anything, to do while the band takes a break.
* Close the bars half an hour before the end of a dance, so that there is a natural wind down and wives get at least the last waltz.
* If local residents object to door slamming late at night, this should be announced in a friendly but firm way to reduce the problem. The toastmaster can do this or the chairman as he bids farewell to guests from the stage or dance floor.

At meetings and conferences

* The chairman should spell out the rules for the function, e.g. whether notes need to be taken.
* There should be someone at the back of the

room to signal, perhaps by holding up a news-
paper, whether the sound level is adequate.

* The chairman or master of ceremonies must
  keep things flowing and tell people what is
  going on; an audience will be more relaxed
  and receptive if it feels 'safe' and knows what
  to expect.
* If it is a hot day, an audience may be more
  comfortable with jackets off; the chairman
  should set an example by removing his.
* A simple code system will tell helpers that the
  chairman is bringing things to a close. If the
  code is too obvious, such as 'May we have one
  last question', you will encourage all the
  guests to head for the bar.
* While delegates are out of an auditorium (say
  at a coffee break) ashtrays should be changed
  but papers should not be moved.
* If most of the guests are strangers at a small
  gathering, hand out sheets of paper (as
  quickly as possible after they have sat down)
  showing the names of people and, if possible,
  the positions in which they are sitting.

It is the chairman's thankless job to control speakers if they
ramble on too long. He can try putting notes under their
noses or tugging at their jackets, but if a bore gets into full
flow there is really not much that can be done other than
vow never to invite him again.

Questions should always be put to speakers through the
chair because this helps to stop temperatures rising. It must
be established if the press is present. Some speakers may
like to sound off about something but will have to guard
against this if they don't want to be quoted. Give the press
copies of speeches, if available, so that they don't have to
take notes but stress that speeches must be 'checked
against delivery' if a speaker is likely to ad lib.

Don't hand speeches out beforehand to an audience; if
you do, they won't pay proper attention.

Finally, have a 'close' for the chairman to bring a meeting

to an end because there should be a formal, clear finale to a function. Obviously, it is desirable to end on a high note so, even if you have been berating retailers for not hitting sales targets, try to encourage them with a few words about the future – perhaps with a glimpse of products to come. At the very least, force yourself to wish them a safe journey home.

Emergencies

With luck you won't have any emergencies but you need to know such things as the evacuation procedure for the venue and where the fire exits are. Also, to keep down noise, check that there isn't a fire drill timed for half way through your function.

'Wallpaper music' may help to calm people if there is a drama. Have a contingency plan if the lights fail; it may help if the chairman makes some crack about 'put another coin in the meter'.

On a less disastrous note, have needles, thread, Sellotape, pins, hammer, nails, etc., available, as well as a first aid kit. You will reduce the number of self-inflicted emergencies if you avoid rearranging the programme or inserting a new item into a function at the last minute.

Someone from the company should have a supply of cash. In an emergency, folding money may get things resolved faster than going through more formal channels.

If there is a disaster in the kitchen at a dinner you can only try to make light of it – perhaps get the band to start earlier and have a dance break before the main course. Keep guests informed; don't let the dreaded slow hand-clap start while they are waiting for their meal.

If you have a disaster on your hands, you may have to change the order of your function and the chairman or managing director will have to ad-lib. If delegates are not getting what they were expecting or if they are unsettled about something, you should clear the air before steering things back on course.

Hecklers and drunks

A certain amount of general heckling may add something to a meeting if it is handled with wit and style; if you are covering a highly controversial topic you must expect heckling. However, fed by the growth of protest groups, more malicious heckling is becoming prevalent and is encouraged to some extent by the media. Hecklers at an industrial relations dispute, or a by-pass scheme, tend to become most strident as television lights come on, and producers have been known to encourage background noises to add atmosphere to a reporter's piece to camera. Whether the media are then commenting on the news, or creating it, is not for this book to discuss; recognise that such things happen and that you may get damaging heckling at your humble little function.

So, step forward the chairman of the meeting, because much depends on him; if he sees that things are getting out of control he should appeal for fair play – an appeal which most of the audience will support. If your meeting is on private premises (i.e. the public only have access with the owner's permission – which covers most venues) then guests are there by invitation only and anyone requested to leave by the chairman must do so; if they don't depart then they become trespassers and your 'marshals' can eject them. If they resist, call the police; they can be arrested for causing a breach of the peace.

Beware that you don't create martyrs. If possible, the chairman should allow time for a meeting to cool down and then continue it; abandonment may be just what the hecklers wanted.

Drunks? Throw them out. Why let one or two people spoil things for the rest?

At the end of the day

* As guests leave, someone should check that coats, papers etc. are not left by mistake. Above all, search meeting rooms for any

confidential material left behind (it happens). Some material should always be kept out of sight of course. Politicians and journalists, for example, may not be overjoyed to read potted biographies prepared on them as a guide for management.

* Send conference material to those who failed to turn up.
* Consider if any follow-up action is needed to ensure that your messages are acted on by delegates, not forgotten.
* Send photographs to the local and trade press; if you have delegates from all over the country, a photograph of each of them with the managing director could be sent to local newspapers to increase your coverage.
* Thank the support staff and, if it is a large function and your budget is healthy, throw a 'thank you' party.
* 'Thank you' letters should be sent to people who have helped, with expenses where appropriate, e.g. to outside speakers.
* If the event was the first of a series, don't relax and assume that the next one will be just as successful; different audiences may have totally different approaches to a function. Sometimes an event will succeed with one audience and not with another; it is a matter of chemistry and you may not be able to control it, nor predict it for that matter. Exactly the same presentation, with the same words and visual aids, may enthuse one audience and bore another; even more peculiar, the audience you expect to be enthused may be the bored one. Obviously, if the first event in a series is unsuccessful you must be prepared to change the running order, slash speeches, cut films and do whatever else is necessary to make things work.

Here's to the next time

The adrenalin will be in full flood during a function and emotions may run high, but as soon as an event is over there may be a tendency to forget all about it and move on to other things. However, if you don't try to evaluate a function, how can you learn anything from it for the future?

Earlier in the book I stressed the importance of audience reaction. Your information feedback should therefore start with your guests; it doesn't matter how much of a warm glow management got from their brief moments of glory in the spotlight on a stage or at the top table at a dinner, if the guests were unimpressed then your event was a failure.

During an event the organiser, or delegated assistants, should make a point of talking to some of the guests to gauge their reaction. Try to approach a cross-section of the audience and feed their comments to one person to collate and analyse. Concentrate on essentials: if 80 per cent of interviewees say that the coffee was cold, well that's easily rectified next time, but if 66 per cent say they failed to understand the new product strategy then you've got problems. In fact the latter example would be serious enough to warrant a personal letter from the managing director, plus action by a fieldforce, to correct the situation.

You may consider more structured research during a conference. For example, you could hand out forms and ask guests to score the various speakers on a 1 to 10 scale; but don't then embarrass speakers by posting their marks on a board – study them quietly after the event. Obviously such research would be inappropriate at a primarily social affair like a dinner.

A few days after a function, mail simple questionnaires to, say, 1 in 10 of your guests. Don't make them too complicated – boxes may be ticked to indicate opinions on various things then, at the end, leave a few lines for 'any suggestions you have for improving our next function'. If you were trying to promote any specific messages your questionnaire should be structured to prove whether you were successful. To encourage replies, promise to put completed forms into a raffle for an appropriate prize.

When seeking opinions, accept that some folk are just natural moaners and will be reluctant to praise anything. However, you do want genuine opinions (at least I hope you do, because sycophantic praise is unlikely to help you very much) so don't reward a salesman for some honest but hard-hitting criticism of management, by sending him to an outpost of your marketing empire.

The final piece of paper in a function file should be an analysis of all the verbal and written market research. The report should list all the points needing correction next time (including the cold coffee) and it should also have a detailed budget breakdown and a record of who actually attended. All this information must be written down; people leave or die, so don't assume the knowledge will be handed down by word of mouth within a company. Having written down the information, keep it in an accessible place and let all departments in the company know that the file exists; information is of little use if it can't be retrieved or used. Obviously, if your next function is some years ahead then the venue vetting process etc. will have to be gone through again, but at least you will have a starting point.

Finally, I suppose management should sit back with the report and decide whether it was all worthwhile. This won't be easy because too much is subjective. How do you evaluate the benefits of the cross-feed of information (and goodwill) between, say, a fieldforce and its retailers, or the lift to company morale after a sparkling banquet? I guess that making such judgements is what management is all about. Good luck.

Checklists

The following checklists show some of the main points organisers need to remember. They are by no means exhaustive and organisers will doubtless add to, or amend, them in the light of their own experiences.

The subjects are as follows:

* Planning
* Venues
* Travel
* Meetings and conferences
* Dinners and dances
* Food and drink
* Sound and light
* Visual aids
* On the day.

Planning

1	Objectives	What really trying to achieve?
2	Messages	
3	Audience	Numbers. Type. Partners? Put different audiences in right order, e.g. retailers before press. VIP list? Foreign guests – translation facilities?
4	When	Any clashing events? Work peaks?
5	Where	See Venues Checklist, p.155.
6	Type of event	Dinner, forum, meeting, conference etc? What mood trying to project? Speeches. Presentations. Booking key speakers. Rough timetable.
7	Organising team	Which department? Who in sole charge? Secretarial support. Inter-company co-ordination. Keeping minutes. Outside organisers? Press officer.
8	Finance	Budget. Fixed, variable costs. Contingencies. Charging delegates? Tax. VAT. Insurance – damage, cancellation etc.
9	Objectives	In all the discussion, have you held on to your basic objective?

Venues

1 Consider image trying to project. Would an off-beat venue be appropriate, e.g. a dungeon?
2 Study hotel and conference guides/brochures. Room sizes. Floor plans.
3 Is venue big enough: coffee/cocktail area to meet in?
4 Co-operative management:unions. Sufficient serving staff. Is someone in charge?
5 Adequate car parking. Will guests have to pay?
6 Access from public transport.
7 Acoustics.
8 Noise: any building work planned in hotel or nearby? Any other functions at same time?
9 Can room be blacked out for film: bear in mind time of year.
10 What equipment available: projectors etc? Vet carefully.
11 Lighting: dimmers?
12 Heating/air conditioning. Any smoke detectors?
13 No smoking area.
14 Seating: quantity and comfort.
15 Stage: strong enough for special product displays?
16 Piano.
17 Dance floor.
18 Adequate and convenient toilets.
19 Dressing the venue: flowers, photographic displays, point of sale, banners.
20 Room for the workers.
21 Rooms for speakers.
22 Catering at odd hours for the workers.
23 Luggage lift?
24 Adequate lifts for guests?
25 Vet worst as well as average bedroom.
26 Suites for VIPs.
27 Photocopying, telex, secretarial services.
28 Computer telephone lines.
29 Power points. Is electricity supply adequate?
30 Access for props/products.
31 Access time to set up.
32 Doctor. Dentist.
33 Book in writing: get written confirmation and be clear on cancellation charges.

Travel

1	Arrivals by road	Adequate parking? Charging petrol expenses.
2	Arrivals by train	Adequate taxis or coach? Function timetable to suit key train times.
3	Coaches	Heating/air conditioning.
4	Luggage	Issue unique labels.
5	Travel abroad	Advise delegates of visas, injections, currency rules, dress, local laws and customs, duty free and shopping facilities. Allow for air delays. Contingency plan if groups get stranded. Paying for headsets/drinks in flight. Reporting times. Special check-in desk. Use of VIP lounge? Travel agency courier/s? Allow acclimatisation time before key function.
6	Booking in at hotels	Special registration area? Welcome desk?
7	Funds for organisers	Travellers' cheques etc.
8	Telephone numbers of key people	

Meetings and conferences

1	Organising and support staff	Uniforms?
2	Chairman or MC	Key to success.
3	Content	Mood? Stick or carrot? Grade importance of information to impart. Avoid information overload. Tackle contentious issues early – don't duck. Keep presentations in balance with audience/messages. Caution with (laboured) humour. Special theme of the meeting? Visual aids, see checklist on p. 161.
4	Rehearsals	Early enough to rearrange order if necessary. Time them (stopwatch).
5	Audience	Keeping out gate crashers. Charging expenses.
6	Splitting audience into groups	On registration? Alphabetically or by sales region or country?
7	Seating	Need accurate floor plan. Boardroom, classroom or theatre style? VIPs. Block off unused seats.
8	Alternatives	Cheaper by telephone or satellite link up?
9	Contingency plans	'What happens if it rains'?
10	Exhibitions	Who trying to reach? Budget. Staffing.

Dinners and dances

1	Organiser	Separate team if part of conference?
2	Guest list	VIPs.
		Invitation cards; specify dress.
		Tickets?
3	Seating	Care with top table!
		Round tables perhaps better than branches off top table.
		Table plans.
		Place cards.
		Company host per table.
4	Table decorations	Gifts for ladies?
5	Graces and toasts	Brief speakers in advance.
6	Toastmasters	Brief firmly!
7	Speakers	Book in writing.
		Brief properly.
		Expenses and fee?
		Book rooms for them.
		Delegate someone to look after them.
		Running order of speakers (best last).
		Contingency plan if speaker fails to arrive.
		Noise control during speeches.
8	Prizegivings	Keep brief. Avoid 'in' jokes.
9	Tombolas and raffles	Watch legality.
10	Music etc.	Band or disco? See acts before booking.
		Lights down for dancing.

Food and drink

Food

1	In house or outside caterers?	
2	Crisps, biscuits	Be original. Must be fresh.
3	'Airline' meals	Possible if time and space limited. Need slick system to clear away debris.
4	Wine and cheese	Cheap and informal, but aim for originality.
5	Barbecues/breakfasts?	Only for enthusiasts.
6	Buffets	Not necessarily cheaper than set meal, but guests can mingle. Watch traffic flow at serving tables. Have some seats available.
7	Dinners and banquets	Discuss plans with chef; stay within his limitations – don't experiment. Time available affects choice. Vary courses, light then heavy. Have rough idea of serving time for various courses, can then see if on schedule. Liqueurs and cigars? Depends on your budget.

Drink

8	Coffee	Standards poor. Work at it. Gaelic, etc., take longer to serve.
9	Tea	Offer lemon too.
10	Alcohol	Scope for fiddling, be clear on arrangements with venue. Simple ordering system for wine if not inclusive. Wine for top table. Beer and fruit cup after dinner, e.g. during dancing. Avoid over-strong measures (drink/drive laws). Essential to have professional serving staff.

Sound and light

1	Acoustics	Panels to improve sound?
2	Electrical sockets	Flex on equipment long enough?
3	Position of microphones	One per speaker, if debate or forum.
4	Position of lectern(s)	Avoid mirrors, wall lights behind speakers.
5	Position of screen	Entry doors at other end of room.
6	Screen height	Place as high as possible.
7	Lectern height	
8	Lectern light	Torch for emergency.
9	Microphones	Stands. Emergency mikes. Roving microphones.
10	Loud speakers	Positioning.
11	Sound operator	Not just hi-fi enthusiast.
12	Lights	Switches. Dimmers. Spots. (Don't light speakers from behind or just from above.) Support towers. Use colour to brighten a dull room. Illuminate danger areas.
13	Use lights to 'signal' to audience	Lights down at start.
14	Disconnect telephones/PAs	
15	Appoint 'noise marshals'	
16	Music	'Wallpaper' music to fill silences.
17	Speeches	Length. Drafting and writing (don't evade contentious points). Liaison between speakers.
18	Can equipment be tidied?	Tape trailing wires down for safety.
19	Multilingual translation necessary?	
20	Have you held on to your messages?	

Visual aids

1	Good ambience in room essential	Flowers, point of sale to 'lift' dead areas?
2	Make sure people can see	Check sightlines from all areas. Black out light if showing films etc.
3	Avoid showing irrelevant information	Visuals must refer to what being said. Avoid information overload.
4	Screens	Position as high as possible.
5	Prompting aids	Yes, but persuade one or two speakers to perform without to add 'life'.
6	Boards, flipover charts etc.	Not for large audiences. Prepare drawings in advance.
7	Overhead projectors	Not for large audiences. Good eye contact. Prepare drawings in advance.
8	Slides	Most popular; most abused. Re-read Chapter 17.
9	Films	Run through before start to check. Humorous films to introduce breaks?
10	Video	People will expect professional standards. Watch compatibility of equipment.
11	Other visual aids?	Plenty of novelty items available, but novelty may quickly wear off.
12	Have professionals to operate the equipment	
13	If venue provides equipment, check it	
14	Have you held on to your messages?	

On the day

1   Timetable/worksheet for all assistants. Radio links between key personnel.
2   Set up early.
3   Brief car park attendants. Reserve space for VIPs and speakers.
4   Signs to venue. Welcome on hotel board?
5   Toilets! Clean? Attendant on duty? Paper, towels?
6   Cleaners to tidy room before start. De-bugging for confidential meeting?
7   Be prepared for early arrivals. Name tags laid out. Coffee available. Heating at right level?
8   Cash float if pay-at-door. Security.
9   Reserve seats for committee, VIPs and speakers. Don't forget the press.
10 Check all equipment.
11 No smoking areas signed?
12 Ashtrays.
13 Water for speakers. Not iced.
14 Double check that telephones/PAs cut off.
15 'Noise marshals' on standby.
16 Keep audience briefed on what happens next.
17 Keep hotel advised of progress. May need to shift refreshment times if under- or over-running.
18 Check speakers' return trains/planes during the function.
19 Keep seating plans updated for dinners.
20 Start conferences/meetings on time, dinners around 15 minutes after time indicated.
21 Remove table numbers when guests seated.
22 Charge glasses for toasts.
23 Prizegivings? Don't turn into marathons.
24 Warn at close if local residents complain about cars late at night.
25 Assume something is bound to go wrong!
26 When it is all over, analyse whether it was worthwhile and keep written records.

Index